PMBOK® Guide Edition Five 200-Question Sample PMP Exam®

By John Tracy

ISBN: 1494984180
ISBN-13: 978-1494984182

This book has been developed as a low-cost alternative 200 question practice PMP Exam® for those studying for the new (Summer 2013) version of that exam, as it has changed to accommodate the 5th edition of the *PMBOK® Guide*.

In my years of teaching students preparing for that exam, through several versions of that test, I've developed strong opinions regarding what makes a good exam question, and what does not. I have also noticed clear trends in the *PMBOK® Guide* as it has matured through five editions, and I recently had the opportunity to formally review the latest edition and provide feedback as it moved from draft to a published state. I have brought that experience to bear in this practice exam, which is tightly aligned with the PMP Exam®'s specification in its construction.

The first thing you'll see is a blank answer sheet, which those of you who like to keep your books in pristine condition may use to record your answers (if you need a 2nd copy, there's another on P41). Next comes the test itself. The last section is the test again, this time with the answers appended for each question. This section shows a process group, knowledge area and specific *PMBOK® Guide* reference point to make the process of learning and re-learning easier for you. The book is capped off with a one page summary view of the answers and their associated process group and knowledge area references.

Do not take this exam unless you have read the *PMBOK® Guide*. In fact, you should read it at least twice, and my suggested order of reading is provided in the table below.

Good luck on your journey. If you have any questions about the material, comments to share, or would like help interpreting your results, feel free to send me an email at jtracli1@gmail.com.

First Reading Sequence: *PMBOK® Guide*	Second Reading Sequence: *PMBOK® Guide*
Chapters 1 - 3	Chapters 1 - 3
Annex A1	Annex A1
Chapters 4 – 10, 13	2 Initiating Processes as listed in P61 Table
Appendix A3	24 Planning Processes as listed in P61 Table
Chapters 11-12	8 Executing Processes as listed in P61 Table
Glossary	11 M & C Processes as listed in P61 Table
Chapter 4 (Re-read, Integration Mgmt)	2 Closing Processes as listed in P61 Table

Answer Template

Question	Answer	Question	Answer	Question	Answer	Question	Answer
1		51		101		151	
2		52		102		152	
3		53		103		153	
4		54		104		154	
5		55		105		155	
6		56		106		156	
7		57		107		157	
8		58		108		158	
9		59		109		159	
10		60		110		160	
11		61		111		161	
12		62		112		162	
13		63		113		163	
14		64		114		164	
15		65		115		165	
16		66		116		166	
17		67		117		167	
18		68		118		168	
19		69		119		169	
20		70		120		170	
21		71		121		171	
22		72		122		172	
23		73		123		173	
24		74		124		174	
25		75		125		175	
26		76		126		176	
27		77		127		177	
28		78		128		178	
29		79		129		179	
30		80		130		180	
31		81		131		181	
32		82		132		182	
33		83		133		183	
34		84		134		184	
35		85		135		185	
36		86		136		186	
37		87		137		187	
38		88		138		188	
39		89		139		189	
40		90		140		190	
41		91		141		191	
42		92		142		192	
43		93		143		193	
44		94		144		194	
45		95		145		195	
46		96		146		196	
47		97		147		197	
48		98		148		198	
49		99		149		199	
50		100		150		200	

Table of Contents

1. When Closing a project, the project manager:

A. Reviews phase closure information to ensure the project has met its objectives
B. Reviews the scope baseline
C. Finalizes any open claims
D. A and B.

2. A project charter aligns the project with:

A. The project manager's work priorities
B. The strategy and ongoing work of the organization
C. The project's scope
D. The project management plan.

3. The key benefit of the Close Procurements Process is:

A. It increases the chance of final acceptance
B. It documents agreements for reference
C. It signals that all project activities are complete
D. B and C.

4. Stakeholders are:

A. Generally at the same levels within a project organization
B. A subset of the project team itself
C. Team members and non-team members, but never the general public
D. Team members and other interested parties external to the project team.

5. Factors influencing make-buy decisions include

A. Associated risks
B. Clarity of vendor proposals
C. Outputs of a multi-criteria decision analysis
D. Level of vendor interest.

6. Managing stakeholder engagement includes:

A. Managing stakeholders via minimizing their impact
B. Locking in stakeholder commitments one time, at the beginning of the project
C. Managing stakeholder expectations by negotiating & communicating
D. None of the above.

7. The Direct and Manage Project Work process:

A. Tracks, reviews & reports project progress
B. Performs the work defined in the Project Management Plan
C. Implements approved changes
D. B and C.

8. Techniques for communications management include:

A. Choice of media and writing style
B. Observation and conversation
C. Listening and facilitation techniques
D. A and C.

9. Disadvantages of virtual teams include all but which of the following?

A. Feelings of isolation
B. Cost of supporting technology
C. Adding special expertise to a project team
D. Difficulty sharing knowledge & experience.

10. The BAC for your project is 33,000 hours. You were supposed to have completed 16,500 hours at this point in time, but you have only completed 45% of the total work, and have spent 18,000 hours in the process. Assuming you have computed your ETC at 17,000 hours, and your EAC at 36,150, what EAC equation assumption did you make?

A. SPI is the best performance metric to use to estimate future performance
B. CPI is the best performance metric to use to estimate future performance
C. I've resolved the performance issues and will perform to budget going forward
D. Adding ETC to actual costs burned to date will yield the most accurate estimate.

11. Examples of interpersonal skills that a project manager uses most often are:

A. Power, Negotiation & Conflict Management
B. Leading, Influencing & Effective Decision-Making
C. Motivation, Communication & Political Awareness
D. Team Building, Trust Building & Coaching.

12. Inputs of the Perform Quality Assurance process include:

A. Process Improvement Plan
B. Quality checklists
C. Work performance data
D. A and B.

13. Objectives of developing a project team include all but which of the following?

A. Improving knowledge & skill of team members to enable project success
B. Improving project member communications with key stakeholders
C. Improving feelings of trust
D. Creating a collaborative team culture.

14. The Perform Integrated Change Control process involves:

A. Reviewing change requests
B. Approving and managing the changes that occur
C. Communicating the disposition of changes requested
D. All of the above.

15. Quality Assurance (QA) and Quality Control (QC):

A. Are synonymous
B. Differ in that QA is about demonstrating acceptance criteria have been met, while QC is about providing confidence they will be met
C. Differ in that QA is used in planning only, while QC is used in executing & closing
D. Differ in that QC is about demonstrating acceptance criteria have been met, while QA is about providing confidence they will be met.

16. In controlling procurements, enterprises:

A. Select sellers and award contracts
B. Often separate contract administration from the project organization
C. Do not concern themselves with project team awareness of legal implications
D. Typically have contract administration report into the project manager.

17. Monitor and Control Project Work is concerned with:

A. Providing reporting on project progress and forecasts
B. Prioritizing customer requirements
C. Decomposing the work of the project
D. Initial risk identification for the project.

18. An Issue Log is used to:

A. Document changes as they occur
B. Provide an historical repository and a platform for subsequent communications
C. Document the impact of changes on a project relative to time, cost & risk
D. Capture rejected changes.

19. The key benefit of the Validate Scope process is that:

A. It identifies the genesis of poor processes
B. It takes actions to eliminate poor process results
C. It brings objectivity to the acceptance process
D. B and C.

20. You want to take a structured look at the effectiveness of your risk response strategies. You have therefore decided to:

A. Conduct a variance and trend analysis
B. Hold an all-team meeting to gather input
C. Do a risk reassessment
D. Conduct a risk audit.

21. Control Schedule is concerned with:

A. Holding firm to your schedule baseline at any cost
B. Influencing the factors that create changes to a schedule
C. Allowing only the project manager to change the schedule
D. A and B.

22. Which Control Process uses Project Management Plan elements such as the life cycle selected, how human resource requirements will be met, and how work will be executed?

A. Control Scope
B. Control Risk
C. Control Human Resources
D. Control Stakeholder Engagement.

23. Project management plan inputs into the Control Scope process include:

A. Cost & schedule baselines
B. The change and configuration management plans
C. Stakeholder communication requirements
D. The selected project life cycle.

24. In analyzing the engagement level of stakeholders, the current engagement levels are compared to desired levels to identify gaps and plans for closing them. Engagement levels for stakeholders include:

A. Unaware, Neutral & Leading
B. Expert, Referent and Legitimate
C. Withdrawing, Collaborating & Compromising
D. Resistant, Supportive & Coaching.

25. Which of the following is true of a definitive estimate (also called grassroots, or engineering estimate):

A. It is generally accurate within plus or minus 10%
B. It is usually based on analogous information
C. It can be prepared quickly
D. B and C.

26. You have been working under a Cost Plus Incentive contract, with a 75/25 share. The target cost and target profit in the contract are $150,000 and $25,000, respectively. The contract ceiling amount is $195,000. Over the course of the contract, the seller incurred $180,000 in actual documented, substantiated costs. What is the total payout for the procurement?

A. $180,000
B. $197,500
C. $195,000
D. $175,000.

27. A RACI Chart:

A. Is a form of an Organizational Breakdown Structure
B. Links the project team members to the work packages
C. Is an acronym that stands for Responsible, Analyze, Consult and Inquire
D. B and C.

28. Information gathering techniques used in identifying risks include:

A. Force field and multicriteria decision analysis
B. Idea/mind mapping and affinity diagrams
C. Interviewing & Root Cause Analysis
D. Cause-and-effect diagrams and flowcharts.

29. A Project Management Plan:

A. Is generally the same regardless of the complexity of a project
B. Is usually fairly static once put into motion
C. Should be consistent with the program management plan that drives it
D. Includes a section on maintenance of the product of the project.

30. Solution requirements are grouped into:

A. Business & Stakeholder
B. Functional & Non-Functional
C. Quality & Scalability
D. Transition & Project.

31. You are bidding on a project that is potentially very lucrative, but involves some new and highly unstable technology. You decide to proceed with the bid, but also price in some insurance with Lloyds of London in response to the risk level. What type of risk response strategy is this?

A. Mitigation
B. Transference
C. Sharing
D. Enhancement.

32. A Schedule Management Plan includes all but which of the following?

A. Rules of performance measurement & control thresholds
B. Level of accuracy & units of measure information
C. Procedures for project cost reporting
D. Project schedule model information.

33. You have been unsure about the use of reserves in estimating, and have sought the counsel of an experienced, certified project manager. She tells you that:

A. Management reserves are part of the cost baseline of the project
B. Management reserves are the budget for the "unknown unknowns" of the project
C. Contingency reserves are the budget for the "known unknowns" of the project
D. B and C.

34. You have just created a document which includes a set of deliverable acceptance criteria, project exclusions and assumptions & constraints. What is this document?

A. Project Plan
B. Project Requirements
C. Project Scope Statement
D. Work Breakdown Structure.

35. You have just take over as project management director for an enterprise that has caught "project management fever" and is looking to you to help them not only in delivering successful projects, but also in redesigning weak processes and reshaping functional staffing allocations. One of the first decisions facing you is whether to install a four-person quality assurance team. You have estimated that investing in this team will cost you $50,000 per year in fully-loaded costs, per team member. Current development processes are yielding 200 defects to the field each year, and each defect costs $2,000 to fix. In addition, per contractual service level agreement, each delivered defect results in a penalty credit of $1,500 to the customer. While the proposed QA Team will not reduce development defects, it is estimated that the team will catch 95% of them before customer delivery. Using EMV Analysis, what is your determined course of action?

A. Total cost with QA Team is $300,000, cost without is $215,000; don't staff QA team
B. Total cost with QA Team is $215,000, cost without is $300,000; staff QA team
C. Total cost with QA Team is $700,000, cost without is $615,000; don't staff QA team
D. Total cost with QA Team is $615,000, cost without is $700,000; staff QA team.

36. Communication Models are important for a project manager to understand in planning communication for their project. As part of the basic communication model:

A. The receiver of the information is responsible for understanding and acknowledging it
B. The receiver of the information is responsible for responding and agreeing to it
C. The sequence of steps in the model is to Transmit, Decode and provide Feedback
D. A and C.

37. Decomposition is used to break large/complex units of work into increasingly smaller, more manageable items. In creating a WBS, the result of decomposition is always:

A. Lower level items of a tangible, verifiable nature
B. Lower level items representing project schedule activities
C. Lower level items broken out by project phases
D. A tree structure with the same number of levels for every branch of the tree.

38. The most common type of dependency relationship found in the Precedence Diagramming Method (PDM), which requires completion of a predecessor before a successor can begin, is called:

A. Finish-To-Finish
B. Start-To-Finish
C. Finish-To-Start
D. Start-To-Start.

39. The term that takes in all prevention/appraisal costs over the life of the product is:

A. Cost of Quality
B. Cost-Benefit Analysis
C. Cost of Non-Conformance
D. Cost of Conformance.

40. A Scope Management Plan includes:

A. Business requirements
B. A process which enables creation of a WBS
C. Quality requirements
D. A and C.

41. Key benefits of developing a project charter include:

A. Defining project boundaries
B. Defining the basis for all project work
C. Providing a way for senior management to formally accept the project
D. A and C.

42. In conducting procurements, a tool used to bring the buyer and potential sellers together prior to proposal submittals is a(n):

A. Proposal pre-evaluation
B. Independent estimate gathering
C. Procurement negotiation
D. Bidder conference.

43. Stakeholders are classified:

A. According to their interest, influence, importance and expectations
B. Because while they're not diverse, there may be many of them to consider
C. Only on very large projects
D. Because placement into categories allows identical treatment of large groups.

44. Managing stakeholder engagement:

A. Helps minimize stakeholder impact
B. Keeps stakeholders out of the project manager's way
C. Monitors overall project stakeholder relationships
D. Allows stakeholders to be active project supporters.

45. The Close Procurements Process involves:

A. Ensuring that all project work is completed
B. Ensuring that the project has met its objectives
C. Updating final results, reviewing the scope baseline and finalizing any open claims
D. Ensuring that the product of the project has successfully moved to a production state.

46. When acquiring a project team, a project manager should consider that:

A. Getting the right staffing is rarely the cause of project failure
B. Negotiation and influencing skills are paramount
C. Constraints may dictate use of alternate resources
D. B and C.

47. Direct and Manage Project Work activities include:

A. Variance Analysis
B. Managing risks and implementing risk responses
C. Earned Value Management
D. A and C.

48. Assuming that your team is one that has begun to work together well, has developed a trusting relationship, but has not yet reached its peak output, what stage of development have they reached?

A. Forming
B. Storming
C. Performing
D. Norming.

49. The key benefits of the Close Project or Phase Process include all but which of the following?

A. It documents agreements
B. It provides lessons learned
C. It is the formal ending of project work
D. It is the trigger for release of organizational resources to other work.

Use the following data for the next two questions:

You have the following set of six project activities, with associated task durations and predecessor/successor relationships.

A: 2 days; no predecessors
B: 3 days; no predecessors
C: 4 days; both A & B are predecessors
D: 3 days; A is a predecessor
E: 2 days; B is a predecessor
F: 1 day; both C & E are predecessors

50. What is your critical path, and its length?

A. ACF; 7 Days
B. BCF; 8 Days
C. BEF; 8 Days
D. None of the above.

51. More content has been added to Task F, extending its duration to 2 days, and your critical path by one day. To make things worse, your boss has told you that the work must be completed in 6 days, at the lowest possible cost. Looking at the table below, which tasks would you crash, in what sequence, and what would your crashing cost be?

Task	Schedule Days	Crashable Days	Crash Cost/Day
A	2	1	1000
B	3	1	4000
C	4	2	10000
D	3	2	1000
E	2	1	1000
F	2	1	2000

A. D, E & F; $4,000
B. F, E & B; $7,000
C. F, A & C: $13,000
D. F, B & C; $16,000.

52. Activity network diagrams used in quality assurance include:

A. Activity on arrow
B. Activity on node
C. A and B
D. None of the above.

53. Appendix X3 was added in *PMBOK® Guide* V4, to highlight the importance of a project manager's soft skills. Which of the following skills are on the Appendix X3 list?

A. Trust Building, Conflict Management & Coaching
B. Power, Leadership and Cultural Awareness
C. Facilitation, Motivation & Communication
D. Meeting Management, Decision Making & Negotiation.

54. When managing communications, your inputs would include:

A. Issue log
B. Work performance reports
C. Change Log
D. A and C.

55. The Risk Management Plan is a significant document with a high volume of content that is critical to managing risk effectively for a project. The plan includes:

A. Roles and responsibilities, revised stakeholder tolerances and reporting formats
B. Budgeting & Timing information relative to risk activities
C. Risk-initiated change requests
D. A and B.

56. Performing Integrated Change Control usually involves:

A. A Change Control Board to review change requests
B. Change control tools to manage the flow and communication of changes
C. Inspection of completed work
D. A and B.

57. Project Management Plan information used in the Control Communications process includes:

A. Stakeholder communication requirements
B. Change Management Plan
C. Roles & responsibilities
D. Project life cycle selected.

58. You are about to undertake identification of stakeholders. What items would you consider as you begin this process?

A. The project management plan
B. The communications plan
C. Procurement documents
D. The risk management plan.

59. The project charter accomplishes all but which of the following?

A. Early identification and assignment of the project manager
B. Enables partnering of the performing and requesting organizations
C. Authorizes the project manager to plan and execute
D. Establishes the project manager's ownership, as its sponsor.

60. When using an agile vs. traditional/waterfall approach, Control Schedule is about:

A. Conducting prospective views in order to correct problems
B. Analyzing the prioritization of work that has been completed
C. Reprioritizing the work backlog
D. Predicting work velocity for the typical three-month iteration cycles.

61. Project management processes closely linked to controlling procurements include

A. Control Quality & Control Risks
B. Plan Schedule & Plan Cost
C. Manage Communications & Manage Stakeholder Engagement
D. Control Communications & Control Stakeholder Engagement.

62. Effective stakeholder management

A. Recognizes that stakeholder influence is highest during latter project stages
B. Recognizes that stakeholder influence is highest during initial project stages
C. Recognizes that the project's sponsor is responsible for managing this area
D. Recognizes that active stakeholder management can increase project risk.
.
63. Variance Analysis as a Control Scope technique:

A. Decides whether corrective or preventive action is required
B. Is equivalent to EVM
C. May indicate potential impacts from threats or opportunities
D. A and C.

64. Which of the following is true about statistical control processes?

A. Attribute sampling determines whether a result conforms or not
B. Variables sampling defines a range of acceptable results
C. Tolerances identifies boundaries of common statistical variation
D. Control limits measures the result on a continuous scale of conformity.

65. Personnel Assessment Tools would include all but which of the following?

A. Brainstorming exercises
B. Attitudinal surveys
C. Structured interviews
D. Focus groups.

66. Work Performance Data

A. Are measurements integrated and analyzed in context
B. Are the physical representation of information
C. Are raw observations regarding about such things as completion status of deliverables
D. None of the above.

67. When monitoring and controlling project work, one of your key inputs will be:

A. Work Performance Reports
B. Expert Judgment
C. Cost & Schedule Forecasts
D. All of the above.

68. A Requirements Traceability Matrix traces requirements for all but which of the following?

A. Production support
B. Test strategy
C. Project scope
D. Product design.

69. Tools and techniques used in controlling risk include:

A. Variance, trend & reserve analysis
B. Information management systems, expert judgment & meetings
C. Inspections, performance reporting & records management systems
D. Forecasting, performance reviews & reserve analysis.

70. Scope verification & quality control:

A. Are the same
B. Differ, in that scope verification is concerned with deliverables acceptance, and quality control with the correctness of those deliverables
C. Usually happen simultaneously
D. Differ, in that quality control is concerned with deliverables acceptance, and scope validation with the correctness of those deliverables.

71. Organizational process assets updated while managing communications include:

A. Industry standards
B. Stakeholder risk tolerances
C. Stakeholder notifications and feedback
D. Marketplace conditions.

72. The Close Project or Phase Process:

A. Establishes procedures for handling early project termination
B. Engages all relevant stakeholders
C. A and B
D. None of the above.

73. The key benefit of identifying stakeholders is:

A. Finding out who your stakeholders really are
B. Its impact on keeping scope under control
C. Identifying the right focus for each stakeholder group
D. Its impact on the communication plan.

74. Agreements define the intent of a project, and can include:

A. MOUs, SLAs and Letters of Intent
B. Verbal agreements or emails
C. Legal requirements
D. A and B.

75. Procurement Contract Negotiation:

A. Always includes the project manager, though the PM may not always be lead negotiator
B. Is always handled within the Conduct Procurements process
C. Can sometimes be an independent process unto itself
D. Is the process of reaching settlement of all outstanding claims.

76. Early contract termination can result from:

A. Mutual agreement of the parties
B. Default of one of the parties
C. Buyer convenience if addressed in the contract
D. All of the above.

77. Tree diagrams:

A. Are synonymous with Decision Trees
B. Are what is used to depict a WBS, RBS or OBS
C. May only be depicted in a vertical structure
D. Always terminate in multiple decision points.

78. You have just finished acquiring your project team, as evidenced by the following:

A. Resource Calendars & Staff Assignments
B. Team Performance Assessments
C. Change Requests
D. Work Performance Information.

79. You were just in a meeting and heard someone mention something called the "100 percent rule". Immediately after the meeting you pulled up Wikipedia to find out what the term refers to. You found that it means:

A. A Decision Tree accounts for 100% of its event probabilities
B. The work at any WBS level should roll up to higher levels so that nothing is omitted
C. BAC equals 100% of the work to be performed, or 100% of the PVs
D. All of the communication channels on a project need to be accounted for in planning.

80. The Perform Integrated Change Control Process:

A. Begins sometime after the project's inception
B. Accepts changes in both oral and written form
C. Often employs a Change Control Board to review/evaluate changes
D. Requires only the approval of the project manager to move changes forward.

81. A Project Statement of Work references:

A. The business need, scope description and strategic plan
B. Project scope that is to be contracted / outsourced
C. Functional, non-functional & transitional requirements
D. The WBS and WBS Dictionary.

82. You are working on a project that is projected to take 12 months to complete. The first three months of activity are very well-defined at this point, but the rest of the work schedule looks very hazy to you. What activity definition technique might you use to your advantage in this situation?

A. Joint Application Design
B. Progressive Elaboration
C. Rolling Wave Planning
D. Decomposition.

83. Analytical techniques that may be used in planning cost management include:

A. Estimating approaches
B. Make-Or-Buy analyses
C. Regression analysis
D. Variance & Trend analysis.

84. Inspections are also called:

A. Walkthroughs
B. Audits
C. Defects
D. A and B.

85. When updating the project management plan in controlling procurements, plan elements that are likely to be updated include:

A. Cost & schedule baselines
B. Scope baseline
C. Procurement management plan
D. A and C.

86. In utilizing expert judgment as part of controlling stakeholder engagement, which of the following would come into play?

A. Industry groups and other units in the organization
B. The PMO
C. Guidance templates
D. All of the above.

87. The Cost Baseline for a project includes all but which of the following?

A. Management reserves
B. Activity costs
C. Contingency reserves
D. Control accounts.

88. Examples of work performance data include:

A. Status reports
B. Key performance indicators
C. Memos
D. Recommendations.

89. Outputs of the Manage Communications process include:

A. Change log
B. Project management plan and document updates
C. Change requests
D. Enterprise environmental factors.

90. Often, a Multi-Criteria Decision Analysis is used to assist in making project staffing decisions. Some examples of selection criteria include:

A. Brainstorming
B. Knowledge & Availability
C. Negotiation
D. A and B.

91. Examples of management skills used in managing stakeholder engagement include:

A. Facilitating consensus & modifying organizational behavior
B. Coaching and conflict management
C. Influencing and team building
D. Negotiation and cultural awareness.

92. It is important to have legitimate power when driving a project. What other type of power does a project manager need to maximize their effectiveness?

A. Referent
B. Expert
C. Authoritative
D. Laissez Faire.

93. Organizational Process Assets inputs affecting the Close Project or Phase Process include:

A. Procurement documents
B. Project or phase closure guidelines
C. Historical information & lessons learned
D. B and C.

94. A procurement statement of work would include:

A. Impacts to entities outside the performing organization
B. Guiding organizational principles
C. Quantity desired & work location
D. A and B.

95. In an early contract termination situation, the buyer:

A. May have to compensate the seller for completed work to-date
B. In all cases, may only cancel the whole contract
C. In all cases, may only cancel part of the contract
D. A and B.

96. After completing your project's stakeholder analysis, you've identified a stakeholder who is highly interested in your project, but has little power to affect it. How should you manage that stakeholder?

A. Keep them satisfied
B. Manage them closely
C. Keep them informed
D. Monitor them occasionally.

97. Facilitation techniques used to guide development of the project charter include:

A. Meeting management
B. Brainstorming
C. Conflict resolution
D. All of the above.

98. Analytical techniques such as reserve, trend and variance analysis are used in:

A. Quality Assurance
B. Monitoring and Controlling Project Performance
C. Control Quality
D. A and C.

Use the following information to answer the next four questions.

You have just been handed responsibility for a project that is well underway. It was originally budgeted at 200,000 hours of work. About 40% of the project's planned value has been created, its schedule variance is 5,000, and its CPI is currently running at .90.

99. What is the cost variance for the project?

A. 2014
B. -8889
C. 8889
D. -2014.

100. What is the schedule performance index for the project?

A. 5000
B. .93
C. -5000
D. 1.07.

101. Assuming that you have corrected the issues leading to your current CPI, what would your EAC for the project be?

A. 210,000
B. 222,000
C. 208,889
D. 212,889.

102. Your boss has seen your latest EAC projection, and is not happy. Being a realist, though, as well as a fan of the TCPI metric, he wants to know what your TCPI would have to be to bring the project in at 3% over the original budget. What is that number?

A. 1.08
B. 1.035
C. 1.07
D. 1.025.

103. Stakeholder Analysis includes:

A. Identifying stakeholders and assessing their potential situational responses
B. Engaging stakeholders to determine their level of project commitment
C. Managing stakeholder expectations
D. A and B.

104. The project charter:

A. Includes change and configuration management plans
B. Formally authorizes the project and the project manager
C. Documents business needs, assumptions and constraints
D. B and C.

105. Communications and Stakeholder Management are very tightly interwoven. The stakeholder register is a key input to communications planning, and the resulting communications management plan is in turn a key input to managing stakeholder engagement. Elements of the communications management plan used in managing stakeholder engagement include:

A. Escalation process
B. Change log
C. Persons responsible for communicating information
D. Charts of project information flow.

106. Outputs of Perform Quality Assurance include:

A. Quality Control measurements
B. Validated changes
C. Change requests
D. Verified deliverables.

107. A stakeholder classification model that categorizes stakeholders based on their power and legitimacy is a:

A. Power/Interest Grid
B. Salience Model
C. Power/Influence Grid
D. Influence/Impact Grid.

108. Organizational Process Assets Updates from the Close Procurements Process include deliverable acceptance documentation. This documentation requires:

A. Retention by the organization, if defined in the customer/provider agreement
B. Information addressing any nonconforming deliverables
C. A and B
D. A Requirements Traceability Matrix.

109. Project managers should:

A. Create an environment that facilitates teamwork
B. Motivate the team via competitive pay programs
C. Not be concerned with cultural diversity, as global sourcing over the past twenty years has worked out most of those problems
D. A and B.

110. Tools and techniques used to manage communications include:

A. Performance Reporting
B. Management Skills
C. Interpersonal Skills
D. Conflict Management.

111. The Risk Register is the working repository for risk management data for a project, and it is critical that it get off to a good start as risk efforts begin for a project. In developing the initial register as part of the first round of identifying project risks, which of the list below would be included?

A. List of potential risk responses
B. Risk probability & impact assessments
C. Risk categorization
D. B and C.

112. A purpose of the Control Risks process is to determine if:

A. Stakeholders are appropriately engaged in the process
B. Contingency reserves need modification
C. Project requirements are in danger of not being satisfied
D. Cost expenditures are in danger of exceeding the budget.

113. Outputs of the Validate Scope process include:

A. Organizational Process Assets Updates
B. Accepted Deliverables
C. Change Requests
D. B and C.

114. The Conflict Management Style that would be least effective if the time constraint is severe and the positions are wide apart on the issue is:

A. Smoothing
B. Forcing
C. Collaborating
D. Compromising.

115. Today's world has become much more challenging due to the many forms of communication coming at the project team member in the workplace, all of which the project manager needs to understand in order to plan and manage communications for the project. Exacerbating this is the research on communications, which has shown that words by themselves typically make up what percentage of the total communication impact?

A. 13-25%
B. 26-37%
C. Under 13%
D. 38-50%.

116. Analytical techniques used in monitoring & controlling project work include:

A. Regression, Causal & Root Cause Analysis
B. Brainstorming & Interviews
C. Run Charts & Control Charts
D. The Tuckman Ladder.

117. Meetings tend to be of all but which of the following types:

A. Information exchange
B. Full-Team
C. Decision making
D. Brainstorming.

118. A good charter will include:

A. Clarification of project roles
B. A Performance Measurement Baseline
C. A Stakeholder List
D. Project Communication Requirements.

119. In Controlling Communications, the experienced PM knows that:

A. It is exactly the same as Controlling Stakeholder Engagement
B. It is the only control process that does not trigger updates to the project management plan or documents
C. Formal Communication Audits must be undertaken periodically to determine the effectiveness of the project's communications
D. In addition to recommended preventive/correction actions, change requests in Control Communications may result in new/revised cost estimates and schedule dates.

120. Work Performance Information from the Control Scope process includes:

A. Which deliverables have been accepted
B. Amount of rework required
C. How scope variances may impact schedule or cost
D. Contract compliance information.

121. You are talking to the contractor building your new home, who was very excited to find out that you are a project manager. You have asked him why there has been no noticeable activity on the site over the last week. He just informed you that a week ago, the foundation slab was poured, and that it must cure for ten days before framing activity can begin. This predecessor-successor relationship attribute is known as:

A. Lead
B. Mandatory
C. Lag
D. Fixed.

122. Control Quality outputs include all but which of the following?

A. Validated Changes
B. Cost & Schedule Forecasts
C. Verified Deliverables
D. Change Requests.

123. A Procurements Audit:

A. Identifies significant project successes and failures
B. Identifies significant project successes
C. Is fairly unstructured in its application
D. Is focused on the project, and does not extend to other organization projects.

124. In conducting procurements, why would an enterprise want to prepare an independent estimate?

A. It lacks faith in its internal estimators
B. It wants to ensure that prospective sellers fully understood the procurement SOW
C. It feels more comfortable with a multi-discipline review team
D. B and C.

125. Your fellow project manager has just stopped by your desk to chat. She sees that you are down in the dumps. When she asks why, you tell her that you're working a very labor intensive project, and are struggling to organize the many types and number of resources. She suggests you use an RBS to categorize your resources hierarchically. An RBS, in this context, is a:

A. Risk Breakdown Structure
B. Resource Breakdown Structure
C. Resource Break-Fix
D. Responsibility Breakdown Structure.

126. A project was budgeted to take 2,000 hours of work. 750 hours have been burned, and 600 hours of value have actually been created. Your SPI is .9. What is the project's SV?

A. 150
B. -150
C. 67
D. -67.

127. Tools & Techniques used in identifying stakeholders include:

A. Stakeholder Analysis
B. Expert Judgment
C. Meetings
D. All of the above.

128. Conditions driving the business need for a project include:

A. Solution or quality requirements
B. Market demand or social need
C. Customer requests or legal requirements
D. B and C.

129. Sometimes, staff members may be pre-assigned to your project. On the list of possible causes below, which would be considered a legitimate cause for pre-assignment?

A. The sponsor has decided to "help" you with some of her favorites
B. As an industry best practice, the PMO determines project staff assignments
C. Similar personalities were assigned to reduce potential friction
D. Specific staff was already identified as part of a competitive proposal.

130. At the beginning of your project, you and your sponsor agreed on acceptable limits for the project's process variables. You are now 3 months into the project. The sponsor is asking you if the variables are within those limits. To answer him, you consult your:

A. Run Chart
B. Control Chart
C. Scatter Diagram
D. Histogram.

131. A Quantitative Risk Analysis technique that uses simulations and probability distributions is:

A. Sensitivity analysis
B. Expected monetary value analysis
C. Monte Carlo technique
D. Expert Judgment.

132. Project management plan updates resulting from controlling stakeholders include:

A. Change & communication plans
B. Cost & schedule management plans
C. Quality & requirements management plans
D. All of the above.

133. Identify Stakeholders:

A. Identifies impactful parties to the project
B. Documents stakeholder interests & interdependencies
C. None of the above
D. A and B.

134. Major components in a contract agreement would include:

A. Constraints & assumptions
B. Traceability objectives & business rules
C. Functional & non-functional requirements
D. Penalties & incentives.

135. You have been told that a project activity will most likely take 10 days. If all goes well, it will only take 6 days. However, if Murphy's law strikes, it could take 20 days. Given this uncertainty, you have decided to estimate the activity using a Beta, or PERT, distribution. You deliver an estimate of:

A. 10 days
B. 13 days
C. 12 Days
D. 11 Days.

136. You are being tasked with a project that is globally sourced. Your first step is to:

A. Send a memo to all prospective team members noting your appointment
B. Prepare a project charter
C. Hire a translator and cultural coach to minimize misunderstandings
D. Ask your sponsor to prepare a project charter.

137. Arguably the most useful tool/technique used in qualifying risk, the Probability and Impact Matrix:

A. Is used in determining risk urgency levels
B. Marries probability and impact to rate risks as high, medium or low priority
C. Is used in categorizing risks
D. A and B.

138. You have just formed a project team, and all but one of its members have worked well together on prior projects. You are relishing the opportunity to hit the ground running, and expect that the team will start at which developmental stage on the Tuckman Ladder?

A. Performing
B. Norming
C. Forming
D. Storming.

139. Tools and Techniques used in the Close Project or Phase Process include:

A. Analytical techniques such as regression & trend analysis
B. Procurement negotiations
C. Records management systems
D. A and C.

140. One of the key Inputs to the Direct and Manage Project Work process is Approved Change Requests. Those change requests:

A. Are always corrective actions or defect repairs
B. Never result in modifications to policies or procedures
C. A and B
D. Could potentially impact any area of the project.

141. Procurement documents coming out of the Close Procurements Process:

A. Are not used as a basis for evaluating contractors in the future
B. Do not include cost and schedule performance data
C. Include stakeholder register information
D. Include contract payment records and inspection results.

142. Conflict is:

A. Bad
B. Avoidable when a project plan is properly put together and managed effectively
C. Always managed using a Collaborative style
D. Inevitable.

143. You have been assigned to a project where your team will be comprised of people that have worked together well in the past. It will involve building and outsourcing, then integrating components into a final solution. You believe that the biggest challenges will be keeping contractors on schedule and integrating their work. Your first step is to:

A. Begin work on the project plan
B. Hold a kickoff meeting
C. Engage the customer in requirements discussions
D. Begin procurement planning for purchased components.

144. The key benefit of the Conducting Procurements process is that it:

A. Increases stakeholder support for the project
B. Aligns internal & external stakeholder expectations
C. Enables effective, efficient communication flow between stakeholders
D. Ensures seller and buyer performance meet procurement requirements.

145. In identifying stakeholders, the expert judgment of all but which of the following groups should be sought?

A. Subject matter experts in the relevant area
B. Stakeholders with low interest and power scores
C. Industry groups and consultants
D. Senior management.

146. Tools and techniques used to manage stakeholder engagement include:

A. Observation and project performance appraisals
B. Communication methods and interpersonal skills
C. Communication methods and information management systems
D. Expert judgment and meetings.

147. Product Analysis and Alternatives Generation are two techniques used to:

A. Create a WBS
B. Collect Requirements
C. Define Scope
D. Define Activities.

148. You are running a project in an enterprise in which the project environment is one where the project manager's role is acknowledged, but you have low to moderate control. What type of project structure is this?

A. Balanced Matrix
B. Weak Matrix
C. Strong Matrix
D. Functional.

149. Control Scope:

A. Ensures that changes are processed through integrated change control
B. Helps to minimize scope creep
C. Is integrated with the other Control processes
D. All of the above.

150. Organizational process assets updated in controlling procurements include:

A. Correspondence and payment schedules
B. Risk and stakeholder registers
C. Record retention policies
D. Financial databases and completed checklists.

151. You have just inherited a project that was supposed to have generated 50,000 hours worth of value at this point, but has only generated 48,000 hours. You have burned 46,000 hours in the effort. Your project:

A. Is over budget and behind schedule
B. Is under budget and behind schedule
C. Is under budget and ahead of schedule
D. Is over budget and ahead of schedule.

152. Quality Assurance:

A. Is the process of monitoring & recording results of quality activities
B. Prevents defects via planning processes
C. Prevents defects via defect inspections
D. B and C.

153. Enterprise Environmental Factors include such items as:

A. Issue & defect management databases
B. Stakeholder risk tolerances
C. Project files from previous projects
D. A and B.

154. The type of information captured in a Stakeholder Register would include all but which of the following?

A. Stakeholder classification
B. Stakeholder communication requirements
C. Identification information
D. Assessment information.

155. The Manage Communications process allows for which of the following?

A. The ultimate disposition of project information
B. The appropriate generation of project information
C. Stakeholder requests for further clarification and discussion
D. All of the above.

156. The Change Log that flows from the Integrated Change Control process:

A. Includes impacts in terms of risk to the project
B. Does not include information on rejected changes
C. Is for project team use only, and not typically shared with external stakeholders
D. A and B.

157. A Requirements Management Plan includes:

A. A requirements prioritization process
B. Stakeholder requirements
C. Products metrics to be used
D. A and C.

158. Group Decision-Making Techniques include:

A. Plurality
B. Consensus
C. Collaboration
D. Compromise.

159. A primary difference in the use of Control Communications Tools & Techniques, versus Control Stakeholder Engagement, is that:

A. Information Management Systems are not used in Control Stakeholder Engagement
B. Expert Judgment does not call on industry groups and consultants in Control Communications
C. Meetings are focused on the project team with Control Communications, and on status review with Control Stakeholder Engagement
D. Interpersonal Skills are used in Control Communications, but not in Control Stakeholder Engagement.

160. You have just finished work on a document that includes a project scope statement, a WBS and a WBS dictionary. What have you just completed?

A. Performance Measurement Baseline
B. Requirements Document
C. SOW
D. Scope Baseline.

161. Analytical techniques that may be used in planning schedule management include all but which of the following?

A. Choosing estimating approaches
B. Detailing processes for fast-tracking & crashing
C. Choosing scheduling methodologies or tools
D. Variance Analysis.

162. In addition to information in the register, the stakeholder management plan provides:

A. Roles and responsibilities
B. Reason for distribution of stakeholder information
C. Methods used to convey information
D. B and C.

163. Quality Control inputs include which of the following?

A. Process improvement plan
B. Work performance information
C. Quality metrics & checklists
D. Change Requests.

164. Manage Stakeholder Engagement outputs include:

A. Enterprise Environmental Factors & Change Requests
B. Project Communication & Document Updates
C. Issue Log & Change Requests
D. Work Performance Information & Change Requests.

165. Dependency attributes include:

A. Mandatory or Discretionary
B. Fixed or Variable
C. Internal or External
D. A and C.

166. Organizational process assets updated by the Controlling Stakeholders process include:

A. Project or phase closure documents
B. Scope, cost & schedule baselines
C. Project presentations and reports
D. A and B.

167. A good project management plan includes:

A. A Change Management Plan
B. Project Calendars
C. Team Performance Assessments
D. A and B.

168. You are working on identifying project requirements. You decide to use a technique that enhances brainstorming with a voting process. You have chosen:

A. Idea/Mind Mapping
B. Nominal Group Technique
C. An Affinity Diagram
D. Multicriteria Decision Analysis.

169. When implementing risk contingency plans, what type of change requests can result?

A. Recommended corrective actions
B. Recommended preventive actions
C. A and B
D. None of the above.

170. You are project managing a team with a total size of 15 members, including you. A week ago, additional critical scope was added that will require you adding 5 members to your team to meet your date commitment, which will not be relaxed. How many communication channels are you adding to the team?

A. 90
B. 85
C. 105
D. 190.

171. Team performance evaluation indicators include

A. Reduced turnover
B. Improvements in skills & competencies
C. Increased sharing of information
D. All of the above.

172. You have been appointed to a team tasked with project selection for the enterprise. In making project selections, which of the following criteria is most critical?

A. Potential benefits to be realized by the enterprise
B. Balancing cost-saving and revenue-producing projects
C. ROI
D. Realism.

173. Quality Management and Control tools unique to assurance activities include:

A. Matrix Diagrams & Prioritization Matrices
B. Cause & Effect Diagrams
C. Pareto Diagrams
D. Control Charts.

174. The Stakeholder Register:

A. Can be discarded once the Risk Register is produced
B. Is produced one time, at project initiation
C. Should be shared freely with all stakeholders listed
D. Should be consulted regularly, as stakeholders may change during the project.

175. Tools and techniques used in controlling procurements include:

A. Expert judgment and analytical techniques
B. Procurement negotiations and independent estimates
C. Payment systems and claims administration
D. Market research and meetings.

176. You have decided to use the critical chain method to manage your project. Your concern is focused right now on managing three non-critical chains in your project network. You are considering:

A. Adding a project buffer to your network
B. Adding feeding buffers to the three non-critical chains
C. Managing the free float on your non-critical chains
D. Managing the total float on your non-critical chains.

177. Configuration Management activities include all but which of the following:

A. Configuration identification
B. Configuration status accounting
C. Configuration scope creep control
D. Configuration verification/audit.

178. Motivational Pioneer Abraham Maslow is typically associated with:

A. Theory X & Theory Y
B. Expectancy Theory
C. A Pyramid-shaped Hierarchy of Needs
D. Theory Z.

179. You are considering bidding on a project that could be a real growth stimulator for your enterprise, but your limited capital resources just won't stretch to meet the requirements. You are considering entering into a joint venture with a larger company that you have partnered with in the past, and that has better capital resources at their disposal. What type of risk response strategy is this?

A. Mitigation
B. Transference
C. Sharing
D. Enhancement.

180. Organizational Process Assets Updates Outputs of the Close Project or Phase Process include which of the following?

A. Closed procurements
B. Final product, service or result transition
C. Project or phase closure documents
D. Procurement files.

181. In planning procurements, which of the following might be used as source selection criteria?

A. Warranty proposed and business size/type
B. Life cycle costs and financial capacity
C. Management approach and understanding of need
D. All of the above.

182. Tools & Techniques used to control schedules include

A. Critical path method
B. Variance analysis
C. Reserve Analysis
D. Inspection.

183. You are Closing Procurements. What are you producing?

A. Project files & phase closure documents
B. Change requests and work performance information
C. Stakeholder notifications and feedback
D. The Procurement file & deliverable acceptance.

184. Three-Point Estimating:

A. Is synonymous with PERT
B. May use either a Beta or Triangular Distribution
C. Uses most likely, least likely and somewhat unlikely estimates in its formulas
D. None of the above.

185. The Human Resource Management Plan includes:

A. Methods or Technologies used to convey information
B. Stakeholder Interrelationships
C. Roles & Responsibilities information
D. A and C.

186. Performance reporting is critical for a project. It involves:

A. Collecting & analyzing baseline versus actual data
B. Providing information at the appropriate level for each audience
C. A and B
D. None of the above.

187. A Cost Management Plan includes all but which of the following?

A. Rules of performance measurement & control thresholds
B. Level of accuracy & units of measure information
C. Procedures for project cost reporting
D. Project schedule model information.

188. When developing a project team, which tools might you use?

A. Networking & organizational theory
B. Negotiation & Multi-Criteria Decision Analysis
C. Team-Building activities & personnel assessment tools
D. Observation & Conversation.

189. A type of audit that identifies nonconforming organizational/project processes is:

A. Procurement Audit
B. Quality Audit
C. Risk Audit
D. Tax Audit.

190. You have just been hired by your company on the basis of your project management certification and years of experience. You have been placed in charge of a critical project. Which power type are you most likely to use?

A. Authoritarian
B. Referent
C. Expert
D. Legitimate.

191. If your project has passed the halfway point with respect to calendar, its CPI is .65, and your SPI is also less than 1.0, you should:

A. Begin replanning efforts, as your original estimates were flawed
B. Begin working to improve productivity and thereby increase your CPI
C. Investigate the impact that maintenance costs are having on your project
D. Work to improve your SPI, as improvements in SPI should have a positive effect on your CPI.

192. In acquiring project team resources, the project management team will typically negotiate with which of the following?

A. Functional managers and other project teams
B. Government regulators
C. Industry groups specializing in estimating or risk
D. Legal experts.

193. In understanding communication management tools, it is important to know that:

A. A primary focus of communication models is to identify & manage barriers
B. A primary focus of communication technology is to identify & manage barriers
C. A primary focus of communication methods is to identify & manage barriers
D. A primary focus of communication models is to ensure information is received and understood.

194. Changes can be:

A. Corrective or Preventive in nature
B. A planned workaround
C. Defect repairs
D. A and C.

195. Organizational process assets updated while managing stakeholder engagement include:

A. Project reports and presentations
B. Project records and lessons learned
C. Stakeholder notifications and feedback
D. All of the above.

196. Use of analytical techniques within the context of conducting procurements can identify:

A. Areas that call for closer monitoring
B. Root cause and project performance forecasts
C. Estimating approaches or optimal financial techniques to employ
D. Overall risk exposure.

197. Stakeholders are typically classified as:

A. Supportive or resistant
B. Existing or future
C. Management or non-management
D. Technical or non-technical.

198. Procurements Negotiations:

A. Employs litigation as its preferred option
B. Sometimes involves mediation or arbitration
C. Is more concerned with the letter of the contract than equitable settlement
D. A and C.

199. You are the project manager of a project that has just completed the concept, or ideation, phase. What are the key artifacts of this phase?

A. Project Plan and WBS
B. Stakeholder Register and Project Charter
C. Communication and Stakeholder Management Plans
D. A and B.

200. Administrative closure of a project includes all but which of the following?

A. Actions necessary to satisfy exit criteria
B. Actions needed to process any early termination of a project contract
C. Actions needed to collect project records
D. Activities necessary to transfer the project's products to their next phase or operations.

Question	Answer	Question	Answer	Question	Answer	Question	Answer
1		51		101		151	
2		52		102		152	
3		53		103		153	
4		54		104		154	
5		55		105		155	
6		56		106		156	
7		57		107		157	
8		58		108		158	
9		59		109		159	
10		60		110		160	
11		61		111		161	
12		62		112		162	
13		63		113		163	
14		64		114		164	
15		65		115		165	
16		66		116		166	
17		67		117		167	
18		68		118		168	
19		69		119		169	
20		70		120		170	
21		71		121		171	
22		72		122		172	
23		73		123		173	
24		74		124		174	
25		75		125		175	
26		76		126		176	
27		77		127		177	
28		78		128		178	
29		79		129		179	
30		80		130		180	
31		81		131		181	
32		82		132		182	
33		83		133		183	
34		84		134		184	
35		85		135		185	
36		86		136		186	
37		87		137		187	
38		88		138		188	
39		89		139		189	
40		90		140		190	
41		91		141		191	
42		92		142		192	
43		93		143		193	
44		94		144		194	
45		95		145		195	
46		96		146		196	
47		97		147		197	
48		98		148		198	
49		99		149		199	
50		100		150		200	

Answers to *PMBOK® Guide* Edition Five 200-Question Sample PMP Exam®

1. When Closing a project, the project manager:

A. Reviews phase closure information to ensure the project has met its objectives
B. Reviews the scope baseline
C. Finalizes any open claims
D. A and B.

Answer:

D. A and B
PMBOK® Guide Reference: 4.6
Process Group: Closing
Knowledge Area: Integration

2. A project charter aligns the project with:

A. The project manager's work priorities
B. The strategy and ongoing work of the organization
C. The project's scope
D. The project management plan.

Answer:

B. The strategy and ongoing work of the organization
PMBOK® Guide Reference: 4.1
Process Group: Initiating
Knowledge Area: Integration

3. The key benefit of the Close Procurements Process is:

A. It increases the chance of final acceptance
B. It documents agreements for reference
C. It signals that all project activities are complete
D. B and C.

Answer:

B. It documents agreements for reference
PMBOK® Guide Reference: 12.4
Process Group: Closing
Knowledge Area: Procurements

4. Stakeholders are:

A. Generally at the same levels within a project organization
B. A subset of the project team itself
C. Team members and non-team members, but never the general public
D. Team members and other interested parties external to the project team.

Answer:

D. Team members and other interested parties external to the project team
PMBOK® Guide Reference: 13.1
Process Group: Initiating
Knowledge Area: Stakeholder

5. Factors influencing make-buy decisions include

A. Associated risks
B. Clarity of vendor proposals
C. Outputs of a multi-criteria decision analysis
D. Level of vendor interest.

Answer:

A. Associated risks
PMBOK® Guide Reference: 12.2.1.6
Process Group: Executing
Knowledge Area: Procurement

6. Managing stakeholder engagement includes:

A. Managing stakeholders via minimizing their impact
B. Locking in stakeholder commitments one time, at the beginning of the project
C. Managing stakeholder expectations by negotiating & communicating
D. None of the above.

Answer:

C. Managing stakeholder expectations by negotiating & communicating
PMBOK® Guide Reference: 13.3
Process Group: Executing
Knowledge Area: Stakeholder

7. The Direct and Manage Project Work process:

A. Tracks, reviews & reports project progress
B. Performs the work defined in the Project Management Plan
C. Implements approved changes
D. B and C.

Answer:

D. B and C
PMBOK® Guide Reference: 4.3
Process Group: Executing
Knowledge Area: Integration

8. Techniques for communications management include:

A. Choice of media and writing style
B. Observation and conversation
C. Listening and facilitation techniques
D. A and C.

Answer:

D. A and C
PMBOK® Guide Reference: 10.2
Process Group: Executing
Knowledge Area: Communication

9. Disadvantages of virtual teams include all but which of the following?

A. Feelings of isolation
B. Cost of supporting technology
C. Adding special expertise to a project team
D. Difficulty sharing knowledge & experience.

Answer:

C. Adding special expertise to a project team
PMBOK® Guide Reference: 9.2.2.4
Process Group: Executing
Knowledge Area: Human Resource Management

10. The BAC for your project is 33,000 hours. You were supposed to have completed 16,500 hours at this point in time, but you have only completed 45% of the total work, and have spent 18,000 hours in the process. Assuming you have computed your ETC at 17,000 hours, and your EAC at 36,150, what EAC equation assumption did you make?

A. SPI is the best performance metric to use to estimate future performance
B. CPI is the best performance metric to use to estimate future performance
C. I've resolved the performance issues and will perform to budget going forward
D. Adding ETC to actual costs burned to date will yield the most accurate estimate.

Answer:

C. I've resolved the performance issues and will perform to budget going forward;
   $36,150 = 18,000 + (33,000 - EV)$; $EV = .45(33000) = 14,850$
PMBOK® Guide Reference: 7.4.2; Table 7-1
Process Group: Monitoring & Controlling
Knowledge Area: Cost

11. Examples of interpersonal skills that a project manager uses most often are:

A. Power, Negotiation & Conflict Management
B. Leading, Influencing & Effective Decision-Making
C. Motivation, Communication & Political Awareness
D. Team Building, Trust Building & Coaching.

Answer:

B. Leading, Influencing & Effective Decision-Making
PMBOK® Guide Reference: 9.4.2.4
Process Group: Executing
Knowledge Area: Human Resource Management

12. Inputs of the Perform Quality Assurance process include:

A. Process Improvement Plan
B. Quality checklists
C. Work performance data
D. A and B.

Answer:

A. Process Improvement Plan
PMBOK® Guide Reference: 8.2.1
Process Group: Executing
Knowledge Area: Quality

13. Objectives of developing a project team include all but which of the following?

A. Improving knowledge & skill of team members to enable project success
B. Improving project member communications with key stakeholders
C. Improving feelings of trust
D. Creating a collaborative team culture.

Answer:

B. Improving project member communications with key stakeholders
PMBOK® Guide Reference: 9.3
Process Group: Executing
Knowledge Area: Human Resource Management

14. The Perform Integrated Change Control process involves:

A. Reviewing change requests
B. Approving and managing the changes that occur
C. Communicating the disposition of changes requested
D. All of the above.

Answer:

D. All of the above
PMBOK® Guide Reference: 4.5
Process Group: Monitoring & Control
Knowledge Area: Integration

15. Quality Assurance (QA) and Quality Control (QC):

A. Are synonymous
B. Differ in that QA is about demonstrating acceptance criteria have been met, while QC is about providing confidence they will be met
C. Differ in that QA is used in planning only, while QC is used in executing & closing
D. Differ in that QC is about demonstrating acceptance criteria have been met, while QA is about providing confidence they will be met.

Answer:

D. Differ in that QC is about demonstrating acceptance criteria have been met, while QA is about providing confidence they will be met
PMBOK® Guide Reference: 8.3
Process Group: Monitoring & Control
Knowledge Area: Quality

16. In controlling procurements, enterprises:

A. Select sellers and award contracts
B. Often separate contract administration from the project organization
C. Do not concern themselves with project team awareness of legal implications
D. Typically have contract administration report into the project manager.

Answer:

B. Often separate contract administration from the project organization
PMBOK® Guide Reference: 12.3
Process Group: Monitoring & Control
Knowledge Area: Procurement

17. Monitor and Control Project Work is concerned with:

A. Providing reporting on project progress and forecasts
B. Prioritizing customer requirements
C. Decomposing the work of the project
D. Initial risk identification for the project.

Answer:

A. Providing reporting on project progress and forecasts
PMBOK® Guide Reference: 4.4
Process Group: Monitoring & Control
Knowledge Area: Integration

18. An Issue Log is used to:

A. Document changes as they occur
B. Provide an historical repository and a platform for subsequent communications
C. Document the impact of changes on a project relative to time, cost & risk
D. Capture rejected changes.

Answer:

B. Provide an historical repository and a platform for subsequent communications
PMBOK® Guide Reference: 10.3.1.3
Process Group: Monitoring & Control
Knowledge Area: Communications

19. The key benefit of the Validate Scope process is that:

A. It identifies the genesis of poor processes
B. It takes actions to eliminate poor process results
C. It brings objectivity to the acceptance process
D. B and C.

Answer:

C. It brings objectivity to the acceptance process
PMBOK® Guide Reference: 5.5
Process Group: Monitoring & Controlling
Knowledge Area: Scope

20. You want to take a structured look at the effectiveness of your risk response strategies. You have therefore decided to:

A. Conduct a variance and trend analysis
B. Hold an all-team meeting to gather input
C. Do a risk reassessment
D. Conduct a risk audit.
Answer:

D. Conduct a risk audit
PMBOK® Guide Reference: 11.6.2.2
Process Group: Monitoring & Control
Knowledge Area: Risk

21. Control Schedule is concerned with:

A. Holding firm to your schedule baseline at any cost
B. Influencing the factors that create changes to a schedule
C. Allowing only the project manager to change the schedule
D. A and B.

Answer:

B. Influencing the factors that create changes to a schedule
PMBOK® Guide Reference: 6.7
Process Group: Planning
Knowledge Area: Time

22. Which Control Process uses Project Management Plan elements such as the life cycle selected, how human resource requirements will be met, and how work will be executed?

A. Control Scope
B. Control Risk
C. Control Human Resources
D. Control Stakeholder Engagement.

Answer:

D. Control Stakeholder Engagement
PMBOK® Guide Reference: 13.4
Process Group: Monitoring & Control
Knowledge Area: Stakeholder

23. Project management plan inputs into the Control Scope process include:

A. Cost & schedule baselines
B. The change and configuration management plans
C. Stakeholder communication requirements
D. The selected project life cycle.

Answer:

B. The change and configuration management plans
PMBOK® Guide Reference: 5.6.1.1
Process Group: Monitoring & Controlling
Knowledge Area: Scope

24. In analyzing the engagement level of stakeholders, the current engagement levels are compared to desired levels to identify gaps and plans for closing them. Engagement levels for stakeholders include:

A. Unaware, Neutral & Leading
B. Expert, Referent and Legitimate
C. Withdrawing, Collaborating & Compromising
D. Resistant, Supportive & Coaching.

Answer:

A. Unaware, Neutral & Leading
PMBOK® Guide Reference: 13.2.2.3
Process Group: Planning
Knowledge Area: Stakeholder

25. Which of the following is true of a definitive estimate (also called grassroots, or engineering estimate):

A. It is generally accurate within plus or minus 10%
B. It is usually based on analogous information
C. It can be prepared quickly
D. B and C.

Answer:

A. It is generally accurate within plus or minus 10%
PMBOK® Guide Reference: 6.5.2 (not specifically referenced, this estimate is the most detailed!)
Process Group: Planning
Knowledge Area: Time/Cost

26. You have been working under a Cost Plus Incentive contract, with a 75/25 share. The target cost and target profit in the contract are $150,000 and $25,000, respectively. The contract ceiling amount is $195,000. Over the course of the contract, the seller incurred $180,000 in actual documented, substantiated costs. What is the total payout for the procurement?

A. $180,000
B. $197,500
C. $195,000
D. $175,000.

Answer:

C. $195,000

The seller recovers his costs of $180,000. Under the 75/25 sharing agreement, he also has to forfeit 25% of the target profit of $25,000, or $6,250, which reduces his profit to $18,750. Adding the $18,750 to the cost figure of $180,000, the total procurement value would be $198, 750; however, the contract ceiling amount of $195,000 becomes the final figure, as $198,750 exceeds that ceiling.

PMBOK® Guide Reference: 12.1.1.9
Process Group: Planning
Knowledge Area: Procurement

27. A RACI Chart:

A. Is a form of an Organizational Breakdown Structure
B. Links the project team members to the work packages
C. Is an acronym that stands for Responsible, Analyze, Consult and Inquire
D. B and C.

Answer:

B. Links the project team members to the work packages
PMBOK® Guide Reference: 9.1.2.1
Process Group: Planning
Knowledge Area: Human Resource Management

28. Information gathering techniques used in identifying risks include:

A. Force field and multicriteria decision analysis
B. Idea/mind mapping and affinity diagrams
C. Interviewing & Root Cause Analysis
D. Cause-and-effect diagrams and flowcharts.

Answer:

C. Interviewing & Root Cause Analysis
PMBOK® Guide Reference: 11.2.2.2
Process Group: Planning
Knowledge Area: Risk

29. A Project Management Plan:

A. Is generally the same regardless of the complexity of a project
B. Is usually fairly static once put into motion
C. Should be consistent with the program management plan that drives it
D. Includes a section on maintenance of the product of the project.

Answer:

C. Should be consistent with the program management plan that drives it
PMBOK® Guide Reference: 4.2
Process Group: Planning
Knowledge Area: Integration

30. Solution requirements are grouped into:

A. Business & Stakeholder
B. Functional & Non-Functional
C. Quality & Scalability
D. Transition & Project.

Answer:

B. Functional & Non-Functional
PMBOK® Guide Reference: 5.2
Process Group: Planning
Knowledge Area: Scope

31. You are bidding on a project that is potentially very lucrative, but involves some new and highly unstable technology. You decide to proceed with the bid, but also price in some insurance with Lloyds of London in response to the risk level. What type of risk response strategy is this?

A. Mitigation
B. Transference
C. Sharing
D. Enhancement.

Answer:

B. Transference
PMBOK® Guide Reference: 11.5.2.1
Process Group: Planning
Knowledge Area: Risk

32. A Schedule Management Plan includes all but which of the following?

A. Rules of performance measurement & control thresholds
B. Level of accuracy & units of measure information
C. Procedures for project cost reporting
D. Project schedule model information.

Answer:

C. Procedures for project cost reporting
PMBOK® Guide Reference: 6.1.3.1
Process Group: Planning
Knowledge Area: Time

33. You have been unsure about the use of reserves in estimating, and have sought the counsel of an experienced, certified project manager. She tells you that:

A. Management reserves are part of the cost baseline of the project
B. Management reserves are the budget for the "unknown unknowns" of the project
C. Contingency reserves are the budget for the "known unknowns" of the project
D. B and C.

Answer:

D. B and C
PMBOK® Guide Reference: 7.2.2.6
Process Group: Planning
Knowledge Area: Cost

34. You have just created a document which includes a set of deliverable acceptance criteria, project exclusions and assumptions & constraints. What is this document?

A. Project Plan
B. Project Requirements
C. Project Scope Statement
D. Work Breakdown Structure.

Answer:

C. Project Scope Statement
PMBOK® Guide Reference: 5.3.3.1
Process Group: Planning
Knowledge Area: Scope

35. You have just take over as project management director for an enterprise that has caught "project management fever" and is looking to you to help them not only in delivering successful projects, but also in redesigning weak processes and reshaping functional staffing allocations. One of the first decisions facing you is whether to install a four-person quality assurance team. You have estimated that investing in this team will cost you $50,000 per year in fully-loaded costs, per team member. Current development processes are yielding 200 defects to the field each year, and each defect costs $2,000 to fix. In addition, per contractual service level agreement, each delivered defect results in a penalty credit of $1,500 to the customer. While the proposed QA Team will not reduce development defects, it is estimated that the team will catch 95% of them before customer delivery. Using EMV Analysis, what is your determined course of action?

A. Total cost with QA Team is $300,000, cost without is $215,000; don't staff QA team
B. Total cost with QA Team is $215,000, cost without is $300,000; staff QA team
C. Total cost with QA Team is $700,000, cost without is $615,000; don't staff QA team
D. Total cost with QA Team is $615,000, cost without is $700,000; staff QA team.

Answer:

D. Total cost with QA Team is $615,000, cost without is $700,000; staff QA team

Decision Tree/EMV Solution

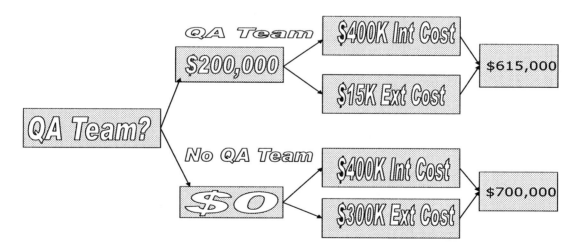

PMBOK® Guide Reference: 11.4.2.3
Process Group: Planning
Knowledge Area: Risk

36. Communication Models are important for a project manager to understand in planning communication for their project. As part of the basic communication model:

A. The receiver of the information is responsible for understanding and acknowledging it
B. The receiver of the information is responsible for responding and agreeing to it
C. The sequence of steps in the model is to Transmit, Decode and provide Feedback
D. A and C.

Answer:

A. The receiver of the information is responsible for understanding and acknowledging it
PMBOK® Guide Reference: 10.1.2.3
Process Group: Planning
Knowledge Area: Communication

37. Decomposition is used to break large/complex units of work into increasingly smaller, more manageable items. In creating a WBS, the result of decomposition is always:

A. Lower level items of a tangible, verifiable nature
B. Lower level items representing project schedule activities
C. Lower level items broken out by project phases
D. A tree structure with the same number of levels for every branch of the tree.

Answer:

A. Lower level items of a tangible, verifiable nature
PMBOK® Guide Reference: 5.42
Process Group: Planning
Knowledge Area: Scope

38. The most common type of dependency relationship found in the Precedence Diagramming Method (PDM), which requires completion of a predecessor before a successor can begin, is called:

A. Finish-To-Finish
B. Start-To-Finish
C. Finish-To-Start
D. Start-To-Start.

Answer:

C. Finish-To-Start
PMBOK® Guide Reference: 6.3.2.1
Process Group: Planning
Knowledge Area: Time

39. The term that takes in all prevention/appraisal costs over the life of the product is:

A. Cost of Quality
B. Cost-Benefit Analysis
C. Cost of Non-Conformance
D. Cost of Conformance.

Answer:

A. Cost of Quality
PMBOK® Guide Reference: 8.1.2.2
Process Group: Planning
Knowledge Area: Quality

40. A Scope Management Plan includes:

A. Business requirements
B. A process which enables creation of a WBS
C. Quality requirements
D. A and C.

Answer:

B. A process which enables creation of a WBS
PMBOK® Guide Reference: 5.1.3.1
Process Group: Planning
Knowledge Area: Scope

41. Key benefits of developing a project charter include:

A. Defining project boundaries
B. Defining the basis for all project work
C. Providing a way for senior management to formally accept the project
D. A and C.

Answer:

D. A and C. B is the key benefit of developing a project management plan.
PMBOK® Guide Reference: 4.1
Process Group: Initiating
Knowledge Area: Integration

42. In conducting procurements, a tool used to bring the buyer and potential sellers together prior to proposal submittals is a(n):

A. Proposal pre-evaluation
B. Independent estimate gathering
C. Procurement negotiation
D. Bidder conference.

Answer:

D. Bidder conference
PMBOK® Guide Reference: 12.2.2.1
Process Group: Executing
Knowledge Area: Procurement

43. Stakeholders are classified:

A. According to their interest, influence, importance and expectations
B. Because while they're not diverse, there may be many of them to consider
C. Only on very large projects
D. Because placement into categories allows identical treatment of large groups.

Answer:

A. According to their interest, influence, importance and expectations
PMBOK® Guide Reference: 13.1
Process Group: Initiating
Knowledge Area: Stakeholder

44. Managing stakeholder engagement:

A. Helps minimize stakeholder impact
B. Keeps stakeholders out of the project manager's way
C. Monitors overall project stakeholder relationships
D. Allows stakeholders to be active project supporters.

Answer:

D. Allows stakeholders to be active project supporters
PMBOK® Guide Reference: 13.3
Process Group: Executing
Knowledge Area: Stakeholder

45. The Close Procurements Process involves:

A. Ensuring that all project work is completed
B. Ensuring that the project has met its objectives
C. Updating final results, reviewing the scope baseline and finalizing any open claims
D. Ensuring that the product of the project has successfully moved to a production state.

Answer:

C. Updating final results, reviewing the scope baseline and finalizing any open claims
PMBOK® Guide Reference: 12.4
Process Group: Closing
Knowledge Area: Procurements

46. When acquiring a project team, a project manager should consider that:

A. Getting the right staffing is rarely the cause of project failure
B. Negotiation and influencing skills are paramount
C. Constraints may dictate use of alternate resources
D. B and C.

Answer:

D. B and C
PMBOK® Guide Reference: 9.2
Process Group: Executing
Knowledge Area: Human Resource Management

47. Direct and Manage Project Work activities include:

A. Variance Analysis
B. Managing risks and implementing risk responses
C. Earned Value Management
D. A and C.

Answer:

B. Managing risks and implementing risk responses
PMBOK® Guide Reference: 4.3
Process Group: Executing
Knowledge Area: Integration

48. Assuming that your team is one that has begun to work together well, has developed a trusting relationship, but has not yet reached its peak output, what stage of development have they reached?

A. Forming
B. Storming
C. Performing
D. Norming.

Answer:

D. Norming
PMBOK® Guide Reference: 9.3.2.3
Process Group: Executing
Knowledge Area: Human Resource Management

49. The key benefits of the Close Project or Phase Process include all but which of the following?

A. It documents agreements
B. It provides lessons learned
C. It is the formal ending of project work
D. It is the trigger for release of organizational resources to other work.

Answer:

A. It documents agreements
PMBOK® Guide Reference: 4.6
Process Group: Closing
Knowledge Area: Integration

Use the following data for the next two questions:

You have the following set of six project activities, with associated task durations and predecessor/successor relationships.

A: 2 days; no predecessors
B: 3 days; no predecessors
C: 4 days; both A & B are predecessors
D: 3 days; A is a predecessor
E: 2 days; B is a predecessor
F: 1 day; both C & E are predecessors

50. What is your critical path, and its length?

A. ACF; 7 Days
B. BCF; 8 Days
C. BEF; 8 Days
D. None of the above.

Answer:

B. BCF; 8 Days

Time Management Network Diagram

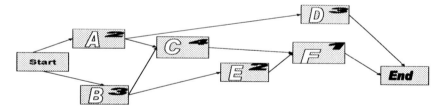

PMBOK® Guide Reference: 6.6.2.2
Process Group: Planning
Knowledge Area: Time

51. More content has been added to Task F, extending its duration to 2 days, and your critical path by one day. To make things worse, your boss has told you that the work must be completed in 6 days, at the lowest possible cost. Looking at the table below, which tasks would you crash, in what sequence, and what would your crashing cost be?

Task	Schedule Days	Crashable Days	Crash Cost/Day
A	2	1	1000
B	3	1	4000
C	4	2	10000
D	3	2	1000
E	2	1	1000
F	2	1	2000

A. D, E & F; $4,000
B. F, E & B; $7,000
C. F, A & C: $13,000
D. F, B & C; $16,000.

Answer:

D. F, B & C; $16,000.

Crashing F first costs $2,000, and shortens two paths currently above 6 days, leaving only ACF (7) and BCF (8) above 6 days. F is now fully crashed, leaving only A, B & C as potential crashable tasks.

Crashing B next costs $4,000, and shortens BCF to 7 days. B is now also fully crashed.

Crashing C next meets the objective of 6 days for the schedule, shortening both ACF and BCF to 6 days at a cost of $10,000. Total cost of crashing is $2K+$4K+$10K, or $16,000.

Note that Task A, which appeared to be a low cost candidate to crash, did not come into play, as the necessity of crashing C and F to reduce critical path BCF by three days also reduced path ACF to 6 days.

PMBOK® Guide Reference: 6.6.2.7
Process Group: Planning
Knowledge Area: Time

52. Activity network diagrams used in quality assurance include:

A. Activity on arrow
B. Activity on node
C. A and B
D. None of the above.

Answer:

C. A and B
PMBOK® Guide Reference: 8.2.2.1
Process Group: Executing
Knowledge Area: Quality

53. Appendix X3 was added in *PMBOK® Guide* V4, to highlight the importance of a project manager's soft skills. Which of the following skills are on the Appendix X3 list?

A. Trust Building, Conflict Management & Coaching
B. Power, Leadership and Cultural Awareness
C. Facilitation, Motivation & Communication
D. Meeting Management, Decision Making & Negotiation.

Answer:

A. Trust Building, Conflict Management & Coaching
PMBOK® Guide Reference: Appendix X3
Process Group: Executing
Knowledge Area: Human Resource Management

54. When managing communications, your inputs would include:

A. Issue log
B. Work performance reports
C. Change Log
D. A and C.

Answer:

B. Work performance reports
PMBOK® Guide Reference: 10.2.1
Process Group: Executing
Knowledge Area: Communication

55. The Risk Management Plan is a significant document with a high volume of content that is critical to managing risk effectively for a project. The plan includes:

A. Roles and responsibilities, revised stakeholder tolerances and reporting formats
B. Budgeting & Timing information relative to risk activities
C. Risk-initiated change requests
D. A and B.

Answer:

D. A and B
PMBOK® Guide Reference: 11.1.3.1
Process Group: Planning
Knowledge Area: Risk

56. Performing Integrated Change Control usually involves:

A. A Change Control Board to review change requests
B. Change control tools to manage the flow and communication of changes
C. Inspection of completed work
D. A and B.

Answer:

D. A and B
PMBOK® Guide Reference: 4.5.2.2, 4.5.2.3
Process Group: Monitoring & Control
Knowledge Area: Integration

57. Project Management Plan information used in the Control Communications process includes:

A. Stakeholder communication requirements
B. Change Management Plan
C. Roles & responsibilities
D. Project life cycle selected.

Answer:

A. Stakeholder communication requirements
PMBOK® Guide Reference: 10.3.1.1
Process Group: Monitoring & Control
Knowledge Area: Communications

58. You are about to undertake identification of stakeholders. What items would you consider as you begin this process?

A. The project management plan
B. The communications plan
C. Procurement documents
D. The risk management plan.

Answer:

C. Procurement documents
PMBOK® Guide Reference: 13.1.1
Process Group: Initiating
Knowledge Area: Stakeholder

59. The project charter accomplishes all but which of the following?

A. Early identification and assignment of the project manager
B. Enables partnering of the performing and requesting organizations
C. Authorizes the project manager to plan and execute
D. Establishes the project manager's ownership, as its sponsor.

Answer:
D. Establishes the project manager's ownership, as its sponsor

PMBOK® Guide Reference: 4.1
Process Group: Initiating
Knowledge Area: Integration

60. When using an agile vs. traditional/waterfall approach, Control Schedule is about:

A. Conducting prospective views in order to correct problems
B. Analyzing the prioritization of work that has been completed
C. Reprioritizing the work backlog
D. Predicting work velocity for the typical three-month iteration cycles.

Answer:

C. Reprioritizing the work backlog
PMBOK® Guide Reference: 6.7
Process Group: Planning
Knowledge Area: Time

61. Project management processes closely linked to controlling procurements include

A. Control Quality & Control Risks
B. Plan Schedule & Plan Cost
C. Manage Communications & Manage Stakeholder Engagement
D. Control Communications & Control Stakeholder Engagement.

Answer:

A. Control Quality & Control Risks
PMBOK® Guide Reference: 12.3
Process Group: Monitoring & Control
Knowledge Area: Procurement

62. Effective stakeholder management

A. Recognizes that stakeholder influence is highest during latter project stages
B. Recognizes that stakeholder influence is highest during initial project stages
C. Recognizes that the project's sponsor is responsible for managing this area
D. Recognizes that active stakeholder management can increase project risk.
.

Answer:

B. Recognizes that stakeholder influence is highest during initial project stages
PMBOK® Guide Reference: 13.3
Process Group: Executing
Knowledge Area: Stakeholder

63. Variance Analysis as a Control Scope technique:

A. Decides whether corrective or preventive action is required
B. Is equivalent to EVM
C. May indicate potential impacts from threats or opportunities
D. A and C.

Answer:

A. Decides whether corrective or preventive action is required
PMBOK® Guide Reference: 5.6.2.1
Process Group: Monitoring & Controlling
Knowledge Area: Scope

64. Which of the following is true about statistical control processes?

A. Attribute sampling determines whether a result conforms or not
B. Variables sampling defines a range of acceptable results
C. Tolerances identifies boundaries of common statistical variation
D. Control limits measures the result on a continuous scale of conformity.

Answer:

A. Attribute sampling determines whether a result conforms or not
PMBOK® Guide Reference: 8.3
Process Group: Monitoring & Control
Knowledge Area: Quality

65. Personnel Assessment Tools would include all but which of the following?

A. Brainstorming exercises
B. Attitudinal surveys
C. Structured interviews
D. Focus groups.

Answer:

A. Brainstorming exercises
PMBOK® Guide Reference: 9.3.2.7
Process Group: Executing
Knowledge Area: Human Resource Management

66. Work Performance Data

A. Are measurements integrated and analyzed in context
B. Are the physical representation of information
C. Are raw observations regarding about such things as completion status of deliverables
D. None of the above.

Answer:

C. Are raw observations regarding about such things as completion status of deliverables
PMBOK® Guide Reference: 4.3 (also, P 59)
Process Group: Executing
Knowledge Area: Integration

67. When monitoring and controlling project work, one of your key inputs will be:

A. Work Performance Reports
B. Expert Judgment
C. Cost & Schedule Forecasts
D. All of the above.

Answer:

C. Cost & Schedule Forecasts
PMBOK® Guide Reference: 4.4.1.2; 4.4.1.3
Process Group: Monitoring & Control
Knowledge Area: Integration

68. A Requirements Traceability Matrix traces requirements for all but which of the following?

A. Production support
B. Test strategy
C. Project scope
D. Product design.

Answer:

A. Production support
PMBOK® Guide Reference: 5.2.3.2
Process Group: Planning
Knowledge Area: Scope

69. Tools and techniques used in controlling risk include:

A. Variance, trend & reserve analysis
B. Information management systems, expert judgment & meetings
C. Inspections, performance reporting & records management systems
D. Forecasting, performance reviews & reserve analysis.

Answer:

A. Variance, trend & reserve analysis
PMBOK® Guide Reference: 11.6.2
Process Group: Monitoring & Control
Knowledge Area: Risk

70. Scope verification & quality control:

A. Are the same
B. Differ, in that scope verification is concerned with deliverables acceptance, and quality control with the correctness of those deliverables
C. Usually happen simultaneously
D. Differ, in that quality control is concerned with deliverables acceptance, and scope validation with the correctness of those deliverables.

Answer:

B. Differ, in that scope validation is concerned with deliverables acceptance, and quality control with the correctness of those deliverables
PMBOK® Guide Reference: 5.5
Process Group: Monitoring & Controlling
Knowledge Area: Scope

71. Organizational process assets updated while managing communications include:

A. Industry standards
B. Stakeholder risk tolerances
C. Stakeholder notifications and feedback
D. Marketplace conditions.

Answer:
C. Stakeholder notifications and feedback (others are enterprise environmental factors)
PMBOK® Guide Reference: 10.2.3.4
Process Group: Executing
Knowledge Area: Communication

72. The Close Project or Phase Process:

A. Establishes procedures for handling early project termination
B. Engages all relevant stakeholders
C. A and B
D. None of the above.

Answer:

C. A and B
PMBOK® Guide Reference: 4.6
Process Group: Closing
Knowledge Area: Integration

73. The key benefit of identifying stakeholders is:

A. Finding out who your stakeholders really are
B. Its impact on keeping scope under control
C. Identifying the right focus for each stakeholder group
D. Its impact on the communication plan.

Answer:

C. Identifying the right focus for each stakeholder group
PMBOK Reference: 13.1
Process Group: Initiating
Knowledge Area: Stakeholder

74. Agreements define the intent of a project, and can include:

A. MOUs, SLAs and Letters of Intent
B. Verbal agreements or emails
C. Legal requirements
D. A and B.

Answer:

D. A and B
PMBOK® Guide Reference: 4.1.1.3
Process Group: Initiating
Knowledge Area: Integration

75. Procurement Contract Negotiation:

A. Always includes the project manager, though the PM may not always be lead negotiator
B. Is always handled within the Conduct Procurements process
C. Can sometimes be an independent process unto itself
D. Is the process of reaching settlement of all outstanding claims.

Answer:

C. Can sometimes be an independent process unto itself
PMBOK® Guide Reference: 12.2.2.7
Process Group: Executing
Knowledge Area: Procurement

76. Early contract termination can result from:

A. Mutual agreement of the parties
B. Default of one of the parties
C. Buyer convenience if addressed in the contract
D. All of the above.

Answer:

D. All of the above
PMBOK® Guide Reference: 12.4
Process Group: Closing
Knowledge Area: Procurements

77. Tree diagrams:

A. Are synonymous with Decision Trees
B. Are what is used to depict a WBS, RBS or OBS
C. May only be depicted in a vertical structure
D. Always terminate in multiple decision points.

Answer:

B. Are what is used to depict a WBS, RBS or OBS
PMBOK® Guide Reference: 8.2.2.1
Process Group: Executing
Knowledge Area: Quality

78. You have just finished acquiring your project team, as evidenced by the following:

A. Resource Calendars & Staff Assignments
B. Team Performance Assessments
C. Change Requests
D. Work Performance Information.

Answer:

A. Resource Calendars & Staff Assignments
PMBOK® Guide Reference: 9.2.3
Process Group: Executing
Knowledge Area: Human Resource Management

79. You were just in a meeting and heard someone mention something called the "100 percent rule". Immediately after the meeting you pulled up Wikipedia to find out what the term refers to. You found that it means:

A. A Decision Tree accounts for 100% of its event probabilities
B. The work at any WBS level should roll up to higher levels so that nothing is omitted
C. BAC equals 100% of the work to be performed, or 100% of the PVs
D. All of the communication channels on a project need to be accounted for in planning.

Answer:

B. The work at any WBS level should roll up to higher levels so that nothing is omitted
PMBOK® Guide Reference: 5.4.2
Process Group: Planning
Knowledge Area: Scope

80. The Perform Integrated Change Control Process:

A. Begins sometime after the project's inception
B. Accepts changes in both oral and written form
C. Often employs a Change Control Board to review/evaluate changes
D. Requires only the approval of the project manager to move changes forward.

Answer:

C. Often employs a Change Control Board to review/evaluate changes
PMBOK® Guide Reference: 4.5
Process Group: Monitoring & Control
Knowledge Area: Integration

81. A Project Statement of Work references:

A. The business need, scope description and strategic plan
B. Project scope that is to be contracted / outsourced
C. Functional, non-functional & transitional requirements
D. The WBS and WBS Dictionary.

Answer:

A. The business need, scope description and strategic plan
PMBOK® Guide Reference: 4.1.1.1
Process Group: Initiating
Knowledge Area: Integration

82. You are working on a project that is projected to take 12 months to complete. The first three months of activity are very well-defined at this point, but the rest of the work schedule looks very hazy to you. What activity definition technique might you use to your advantage in this situation?

A. Joint Application Design
B. Progressive Elaboration
C. Rolling Wave Planning
D. Decomposition.

Answer:

C. Rolling Wave Planning
PMBOK® Guide Reference: 6.2.2.2
Process Group: Planning
Knowledge Area: Time

83. Analytical techniques that may be used in planning cost management include:

A. Estimating approaches
B. Make-Or-Buy analyses
C. Regression analysis
D. Variance & Trend analysis.

Answer:

B. Make-Or-Buy analyses
PMBOK® Guide Reference: 7.1.2.2
Process Group: Planning
Knowledge Area: Cost

84. Inspections are also called:

A. Walkthroughs
B. Audits
C. Defects
D. A and B.

Answer:

D. A and B
PMBOK® Guide Reference: 8.3.2.3
Process Group: Monitoring & Control
Knowledge Area: Quality

85. When updating the project management plan in controlling procurements, plan elements that are likely to be updated include:

A. Cost & schedule baselines
B. Scope baseline
C. Procurement management plan
D. A and C.

Answer:

D. A and C
PMBOK® Guide Reference: 12.3.3.3
Process Group: Monitoring & Control
Knowledge Area: Procurement

86. In utilizing expert judgment as part of controlling stakeholder engagement, which of the following would come into play?

A. Industry groups and other units in the organization
B. The PMO
C. Guidance templates
D. All of the above.

Answer:

A. Industry groups and other units in the organization
PMBOK® Guide Reference: 13.4.2.2
Process Group: Monitoring & Control
Knowledge Area: Stakeholder

87. The Cost Baseline for a project includes all but which of the following?

A. Management reserves
B. Activity costs
C. Contingency reserves
D. Control accounts.

Answer:

A. Management reserves
PMBOK® Guide Reference: 7.3.3.1 (Figure 7-8)
Process Group: Planning
Knowledge Area: Cost

88. Examples of work performance data include:

A. Status reports
B. Key performance indicators
C. Memos
D. Recommendations.

Answer:

B. Key performance indicators (the other three are work performance reports).
PMBOK® Guide Reference: 4.3.3.2
Process Group: Executing
Knowledge Area: Integration

89. Outputs of the Manage Communications process include:

A. Change log
B. Project management plan and document updates
C. Change requests
D. Enterprise environmental factors.

Answer:

B. Project management plan and document updates
PMBOK® Guide Reference: 10.2.3
Process Group: Executing
Knowledge Area: Communication

90. Often, a Multi-Criteria Decision Analysis is used to assist in making project staffing decisions. Some examples of selection criteria include:

A. Brainstorming
B. Knowledge & Availability
C. Negotiation
D. A and B.

Answer:

B. Knowledge & Availability
PMBOK® Guide Reference: 9.2.2.5
Process Group: Executing
Knowledge Area: Human Resource Management

91. Examples of management skills used in managing stakeholder engagement include:

A. Facilitating consensus & modifying organizational behavior
B. Coaching and conflict management
C. Influencing and team building
D. Negotiation and cultural awareness.

Answer:

A. Facilitating consensus & modifying organizational behavior
PMBOK® Guide Reference: 13.3.2.3
Process Group: Executing
Knowledge Area: Stakeholder

92. It is important to have legitimate power when driving a project. What other type of power does a project manager need to maximize their effectiveness?

A. Referent
B. Expert
C. Authoritative
D. Laissez Faire.

Answer:

B. Expert
PMBOK® Guide Reference: No specific reference. Know how to apply your power types!
Process Group: Executing
Knowledge Area: Human Resource Management

93. Organizational Process Assets inputs affecting the Close Project or Phase Process include:

A. Procurement documents
B. Project or phase closure guidelines
C. Historical information & lessons learned
D. B and C.

Answer:

D. B and C
PMBOK® Guide Reference: 4.6.1
Process Group: Closing
Knowledge Area: Integration

94. A procurement statement of work would include:

A. Impacts to entities outside the performing organization
B. Guiding organizational principles
C. Quantity desired & work location
D. A and B.

Answer:
C. Quantity desired & work location
PMBOK® Guide Reference: 12.2.1.7
Process Group: Executing
Knowledge Area: Procurement

95. In an early contract termination situation, the buyer:

A. May have to compensate the seller for completed work to-date
B. In all cases, may only cancel the whole contract
C. In all cases, may only cancel part of the contract
D. A and B.

Answer:

A. May have to compensate the seller for completed work to-date
PMBOK® Guide Reference: 12.4
Process Group: Closing
Knowledge Area: Procurements

96. After completing your project's stakeholder analysis, you've identified a stakeholder who is highly interested in your project, but has little power to affect it. How should you manage that stakeholder?

A. Keep them satisfied
B. Manage them closely
C. Keep them informed
D. Monitor them occasionally.

Answer:

C. Keep them informed
PMBOK® Guide Reference: 13.1.2.1
Process Group: Initiating
Knowledge Area: Stakeholder

97. Facilitation techniques used to guide development of the project charter include:

A. Meeting management
B. Brainstorming
C. Conflict resolution
D. All of the above.

Answer:

D. All of the above
PMBOK® Guide Reference: 4.1.2.2
Process Group: Initiating
Knowledge Area: Integration

98. Analytical techniques such as reserve, trend and variance analysis are used in:

A. Quality Assurance
B. Monitoring and Controlling Project Performance
C. Control Quality
D. A and C.

Answer:

B. Monitoring and Controlling Project Performance
PMBOK® Guide Reference: 4.4.2.2
Process Group: Monitoring & Control
Knowledge Area: Integration

Use the following information to answer the next four questions.

You have just been handed responsibility for a project that is well underway. It was originally budgeted at 200,000 hours of work. About 40% of the project's planned value has been created, its schedule variance is 5,000, and its CPI is currently running at .90.

99. What is the cost variance for the project?

A. 2014
B. -8889
C. 8889
D. -2014.

Answer:

B. -8889. EV is .4(200,000), or 80,000. AC = EV/CPI, or 80,000/.9, or 88,889. CV = EV – AC, or 80,000 – 88,889, or -8889.
PMBOK® Guide Reference: 7.4.2; Table 7-1
Process Group: Monitoring & Controlling
Knowledge Area: Cost

100. What is the schedule performance index for the project?

A. 5000
B. .93
C. -5000
D. 1.07.

Answer:

D. 1.07. PV = EV – SV, or 80,000 – 5,000, or 75,000. SPI = EV/PV, or 80,000/75,000, or 1.07.
PMBOK® Guide Reference: 7.4.2; Table 7-1
Process Group: Monitoring & Controlling
Knowledge Area: Cost

101. Assuming that you have corrected the issues leading to your current CPI, what would your EAC for the project be?

A. 210,000
B. 222,000
C. 208,889
D. 212,889.

Answer:

C. 208,889. Formula is AC + (BAC-EV), or 88,889 + (200,000 – 80,000), or 208,889.
PMBOK® Guide Reference: 7.4.2; Table 7-1
Process Group: Monitoring & Controlling
Knowledge Area: Cost

102. Your boss has seen your latest EAC projection, and is not happy. Being a realist, though, as well as a fan of the TCPI metric, he wants to know what your TCPI would have to be to bring the project in at 3% over the original budget. What is that number?

A. 1.08
B. 1.035
C. 1.07
D. 1.025.

Answer:

D. 1.025. Formula is (BAC - EV)/(EACrev – AC), or (200,000-80,000)/(206,000-88,889), or 120,000/117,111, or 1.025.
PMBOK® Guide Reference: 7.4.2; Table 7-1
Process Group: Monitoring & Controlling
Knowledge Area: Cost

103. Stakeholder Analysis includes:

A. Identifying stakeholders and assessing their potential situational responses
B. Engaging stakeholders to determine their level of project commitment
C. Managing stakeholder expectations
D. A and B.

Answer:

A. Identifying stakeholders and assessing their potential situational responses
PMBOK® Guide Reference: 13.1.2.1
Process Group: Initiating
Knowledge Area: Stakeholder

104. The project charter:

A. Includes change and configuration management plans
B. Formally authorizes the project and the project manager
C. Documents business needs, assumptions and constraints
D. B and C.

Answer:

D. B and C
PMBOK® Guide Reference: 4.1.3.1
Process Group: Initiating
Knowledge Area: Integration

105. Communications and Stakeholder Management are very tightly interwoven. The stakeholder register is a key input to communications planning, and the resulting communications management plan is in turn a key input to managing stakeholder engagement. Elements of the communications management plan used in managing stakeholder engagement include:

A. Escalation process
B. Change log
C. Persons responsible for communicating information
D. Charts of project information flow.

Answer:

A. Escalation process
PMBOK® Guide Reference: 13.3.1.2
Process Group: Executing
Knowledge Area: Stakeholder

106. Outputs of Perform Quality Assurance include:

A. Quality Control measurements
B. Validated changes
C. Change requests
D. Verified deliverables.

Answer:

C. Change requests
PMBOK® Guide Reference: 8.2.3
Process Group: Executing
Knowledge Area: Quality

107. A stakeholder classification model that categorizes stakeholders based on their power and legitimacy is a:

A. Power/Interest Grid
B. Salience Model
C. Power/Influence Grid
D. Influence/Impact Grid.

Answer:

B. Salience Model
PMBOK® Guide Reference: 13.1.2.1
Process Group: Initiating
Knowledge Area: Stakeholder

108. Organizational Process Assets Updates from the Close Procurements Process include deliverable acceptance documentation. This documentation requires:

A. Retention by the organization, if defined in the customer/provider agreement
B. Information addressing any nonconforming deliverables
C. A and B
D. A Requirements Traceability Matrix.

Answer:

C. A and B
PMBOK® Guide Reference: 12.4.3.2
Process Group: Closing
Knowledge Area: Procurements

109. Project managers should:

A. Create an environment that facilitates teamwork
B. Motivate the team via competitive pay programs
C. Not be concerned with cultural diversity, as global sourcing over the past twenty years has worked out most of those problems
D. A and B.

Answer:

A. Create an environment that facilitates teamwork
PMBOK® Guide Reference: 9.3
Process Group: Executing
Knowledge Area: Human Resource Management

110. Tools and techniques used to manage communications include:

A. Performance Reporting
B. Management Skills
C. Interpersonal Skills
D. Conflict Management.

Answer:

A. Performance Reporting
PMBOK® Guide Reference: 10.2.2
Process Group: Executing
Knowledge Area: Communication

111. The Risk Register is the working repository for risk management data for a project, and it is critical that it get off to a good start as risk efforts begin for a project. In developing the initial register as part of the first round of identifying project risks, which of the list below would be included?

A. List of potential risk responses
B. Risk probability & impact assessments
C. Risk categorization
D. B and C.

Answer:

A. List of potential risk responses
PMBOK® Guide Reference: 11.2.3.1
Process Group: Planning
Knowledge Area: Risk

112. A purpose of the Control Risks process is to determine if:

A. Stakeholders are appropriately engaged in the process
B. Contingency reserves need modification
C. Project requirements are in danger of not being satisfied
D. Cost expenditures are in danger of exceeding the budget.

Answer:

B. Contingency reserves need modification
PMBOK® Guide Reference: 11.6
Process Group: Monitoring & Control
Knowledge Area: Risk

113. Outputs of the Validate Scope process include:

A. Organizational Process Assets Updates
B. Accepted Deliverables
C. Change Requests
D. B and C.

Answer:

D. B and C
PMBOK® Guide Reference: 5.5.3
Process Group: Monitoring & Controlling
Knowledge Area: Scope

114. The Conflict Management Style that would be least effective if the time constraint is severe and the positions are wide apart on the issue is:

A. Smoothing
B. Forcing
C. Collaborating
D. Compromising.

Answer:

C. Collaborating
PMBOK® Guide Reference: 9.4.2.3
Process Group: Executing
Knowledge Area: Human Resource Management

115. Today's world has become much more challenging due to the many forms of communication coming at the project team member in the workplace, all of which the project manager needs to understand in order to plan & manage project communications. Adding to this is the research on communications, which has shown that words by themselves typically make up what percentage of the total communication impact?

A. 13-25%
B. 26-37%
C. Under 13%
D. 38-50%.

Answer:

C. Under 13%
PMBOK® Guide Reference: No specific reference – research has consistently shown this!
Process Group: Planning
Knowledge Area: Communication

116. Analytical techniques used in monitoring & controlling project work include:

A. Regression, Causal & Root Cause Analysis
B. Brainstorming & Interviews
C. Run Charts & Control Charts
D. The Tuckman Ladder.

Answer:

A. Regression, Causal & Root Analysis
PMBOK® Guide Reference: 4.4.2.2
Process Group: Monitoring & Control
Knowledge Area: Integration

117. Meetings tend to be of all but which of the following types:

A. Information exchange
B. Full-Team
C. Decision making
D. Brainstorming.

Answer:

B. Full-Team (Full Team meetings fall into one of the other three categories)
PMBOK® Guide Reference: 4.3.2.3
Process Group: Executing
Knowledge Area: Integration

118. A good charter will include:

A. Clarification of project roles
B. A Performance Measurement Baseline
C. A Stakeholder List
D. Project Communication Requirements.

Answer:

C. A Stakeholder List
PMBOK® Guide Reference: 4.1.3.1
Process Group: Initiating
Knowledge Area: Integration

119. In Controlling Communications, the experienced PM knows that:

A. It is exactly the same as Controlling Stakeholder Engagement
B. It is the only control process that does not trigger updates to the project management plan or documents
C. Formal Communication Audits must be undertaken periodically to determine the effectiveness of the project's communications
D. In addition to recommended preventive/correction actions, change requests in Control Communications may result in new/revised cost estimates and schedule dates.

Answer:

D. In addition to recommended preventive/correction actions, change requests in Control Communications may result in new/revised cost estimates and schedule dates
PMBOK® Guide Reference: 10.3.3.2
Process Group: Monitoring & Control
Knowledge Area: Communications

120. Work Performance Information from the Control Scope process includes:

A. Which deliverables have been accepted
B. Amount of rework required
C. How scope variances may impact schedule or cost
D. Contract compliance information.

Answer:

C. How scope variances may impact schedule or cost
PMBOK® Guide Reference: 5.6.3.1
Process Group: Monitoring & Controlling
Knowledge Area: Scope

121. You are talking to the contractor building your new home, who was very excited to find out that you are a project manager. You have asked him why there has been no noticeable activity on the site over the last week. He just informed you that a week ago, the foundation slab was poured, and that it must cure for ten days before framing activity can begin. This predecessor-successor relationship attribute is known as:

A. Lead
B. Mandatory
C. Lag
D. Fixed.

Answer:

C. Lag
PMBOK® Guide Reference: 6.3.2.3
Process Group: Planning
Knowledge Area: Time

122. Control Quality outputs include all but which of the following?

A. Validated Changes
B. Cost & Schedule Forecasts
C. Verified Deliverables
D. Change Requests.

Answer:

B. Cost & Schedule Forecasts
PMBOK® Guide Reference: 8.3.3
Process Group: Monitoring & Control
Knowledge Area: Quality

123. A Procurement Audit:

A. Identifies significant project successes and failures
B. Identifies significant project successes
C. Is fairly unstructured in its application
D. Is focused on the project, and does not extend to other organizational projects.

Answer:

A. Identifies significant project successes and failures
PMBOK® Guide Reference: 12.4.2.1
Process Group: Closing
Knowledge Area: Procurements

124. In conducting procurements, why would an enterprise want to prepare an independent estimate?

A. It lacks faith in its internal estimators
B. It wants to ensure that prospective sellers fully understood the procurement SOW
C. It feels more comfortable with a multi-discipline review team
D. B and C.

Answer:

B. It wants to ensure that prospective sellers fully understood the procurement SOW
PMBOK® Guide Reference: 12.2.2.3
Process Group: Executing
Knowledge Area: Procurement

125. Your fellow PM has just stopped by your desk to chat. She sees that you are down in the dumps. When she asks why, you tell her that you're working a very labor intensive project, and struggling to organize the many types and number of resources. She suggests you use an RBS to categorize your resources hierarchically. An RBS, in this context, is a:

A. Risk Breakdown Structure
B. Resource Breakdown Structure
C. Resource Break-Fix
D. Responsibility Breakdown Structure.

Answer:

B. Resource Breakdown Structure
PMBOK® Guide Reference: 6.4.3.2
Process Group: Planning
Knowledge Area: Time

126. A project was budgeted to take 2,000 hours of work. 750 hours have been burned, and 600 hours of value have actually been created. Your SPI is .9. What is the project's SV?

A. 150
B. -150
C. 67
D. -67.

Answer:

D. -67. SV = EV – PV. EV = 600; PV = EV/SPI = 600/.9 = 667. 600 - 667 = -67.
PMBOK® Guide Reference: 6.7.2.1; Table 7-1
Process Group: Planning
Knowledge Area: Time

127. Tools & Techniques used in identifying stakeholders include:

A. Stakeholder Analysis
B. Expert Judgment
C. Meetings
D. All of the above.

Answer:

D. All of the above
PMBOK® Guide Reference: 13.1.2
Process Group: Initiating
Knowledge Area: Stakeholder

128. Conditions driving the business need for a project include:

A. Solution or quality requirements
B. Market demand or social need
C. Customer requests or legal requirements
D. B and C.

Answer: D. B and C
PMBOK® Guide Reference: 4.1.1.2
Process Group: Initiating
Knowledge Area: Integration

129. Sometimes, staff members may be pre-assigned to your project. On the list of possible causes below, which would be considered a legitimate cause for pre-assignment?

A. The sponsor has decided to "help" you with some of her favorites
B. As an industry best practice, the PMO determines project staff assignments
C. Similar personalities were assigned to reduce potential friction
D. Specific staff was already identified as part of a competitive proposal.

Answer:

D. Specific staff was already identified as part of a competitive proposal
PMBOK® Guide Reference: 9.2
Process Group: Executing
Knowledge Area: Human Resource Management

130. At the beginning of your project, you and your sponsor agreed on acceptable limits for the project's process variables. You are now 3 months into the project. The sponsor is asking you if the variables are within those limits. To answer him, you consult your:

A. Run Chart
B. Control Chart
C. Scatter Diagram
D. Histogram.

Answer:

B. Control Chart
PMBOK® Guide Reference: 8.1.2.3
Process Group: Planning
Knowledge Area: Quality

131. A Quantitative Risk Analysis technique that uses simulations and probability distributions is:

A. Sensitivity analysis
B. Expected monetary value analysis
C. Monte Carlo technique
D. Expert Judgment.

Answer:

C. Monte Carlo technique
PMBOK® Guide Reference: 11.4.2
Process Group: Planning
Knowledge Area: Risk

132. Project management plan updates resulting from controlling stakeholders include:

A. Change & communication plans
B. Cost & schedule management plans
C. Quality & requirements management plans
D. All of the above.

Answer:

D. All of the above
PMBOK® Guide Reference: 13.4.3.3
Process Group: Monitoring & Control
Knowledge Area: Stakeholder

133. Identify Stakeholders:

A. Identifies impactful parties to the project
B. Documents stakeholder interests & interdependencies
C. None of the above
D. A and B.

Answer:

D. A and B
PMBOK® Guide Reference: 13.1
Process Group: Initiating
Knowledge Area: Stakeholder

134. Major components in a contract agreement would include:

A. Constraints & assumptions
B. Traceability objectives & business rules
C. Functional & non-functional requirements
D. Penalties & incentives.

Answer:

D. Penalties & incentives
PMBOK® Guide Reference: 12.2.3.2
Process Group: Executing
Knowledge Area: Procurement

135. You have been told that a project activity will most likely take 10 days. If all goes well, it will only take 6 days. However, if Murphy's law strikes, it could take 20 days. Given this uncertainty, you have decided to estimate the activity using a Beta, or PERT, distribution. You deliver an estimate of:

A. 10 days
B. 13 days
C. 12 Days
D. 11 Days.

Answer:

D. 11 Days
PMBOK® Guide Reference: 6.5.2.4
Process Group: Planning
Knowledge Area: Time

136. You are being tasked with a project that is globally sourced. Your first step is to:

A. Send a memo to all prospective team members noting your appointment
B. Prepare a project charter
C. Hire a translator and cultural coach to minimize misunderstandings
D. Ask your sponsor to prepare a project charter.

Answer:

D. Ask your sponsor to prepare a project charter
PMBOK® Guide Reference: No specific reference. The sponsor owns the charter!
Process Group: Initiating
Knowledge Area: Integration

137. Arguably the most useful tool/technique used in qualifying risk, the Probability and Impact Matrix:

A. Is used in determining risk urgency levels
B. Marries probability and impact to rate risks as high, medium or low priority
C. Is used in categorizing risks
D. A and B.

Answer:

B. Marries probability and impact to rate risks as high, medium or low priority
PMBOK® Guide Reference: 11.3.2.1
Process Group: Planning
Knowledge Area: Risk

138. You have just formed a project team, and all but one of its members have worked well together on prior projects. You are relishing the opportunity to hit the ground running, and expect that the team will start at which developmental stage on the Tuckman Ladder?

A. Performing
B. Norming
C. Forming
D. Storming.

Answer:

C. Forming
PMBOK® Guide Reference: 9.3.2.3
Process Group: Executing
Knowledge Area: Human Resource Management

139. Tools and Techniques used in the Close Project or Phase Process include:

A. Analytical techniques such as regression & trend analysis
B. Procurement negotiations
C. Records management systems
D. A and C.

Answer:

A. Analytical techniques such as regression & trend analysis
PMBOK® Guide Reference: 4.6.2
Process Group: Closing
Knowledge Area: Integration

140. One of the key Inputs to the Direct and Manage Project Work process is Approved Change Requests. Those change requests:

A. Are always corrective actions or defect repairs
B. Never result in modifications to policies or procedures
C. A and B
D. Could potentially impact any area of the project.

Answer:

D. Could potentially impact any area of the project
PMBOK® Guide Reference: 4.3.1.2
Process Group: Executing
Knowledge Area: Integration

141. Procurement documents coming out of the Close Procurements Process:

A. Are not used as a basis for evaluating contractors in the future
B. Do not include cost and schedule performance data
C. Include stakeholder register information
D. Include contract payment records and inspection results.

Answer:

D. Include contract payment records and inspection results
PMBOK® Guide Reference: 12.4.1.2
Process Group: Closing
Knowledge Area: Procurements

142. Conflict is:

A. Bad
B. Avoidable when a project plan is properly put together and managed effectively
C. Always managed using a Collaborative style
D. Inevitable.

Answer:

D. Inevitable
PMBOK® Guide Reference: 9.4.2.3
Process Group: Executing
Knowledge Area: Human Resource Management

143. You have been assigned to a project where your team will be comprised of people that have worked together well in the past. It will involve building and outsourcing, then integrating components into a final solution. You believe that the biggest challenges will be keeping contractors on schedule and integrating their work. Your first step is to:

A. Begin work on the project plan
B. Hold a kickoff meeting
C. Engage the customer in requirements discussions
D. Begin procurement planning for purchased components.

Answer:

B. Hold a kickoff meeting
PMBOK® Guide Reference: No specific reference. The kickoff meeting is always the first step, even when team members are familiar with each other, because every project is unique in some respect.
Process Group: Initiating
Knowledge Area: Integration

144. The key benefit of the Conducting Procurements process is that it:

A. Increases stakeholder support for the project
B. Aligns internal & external stakeholder expectations
C. Enables effective, efficient communication flow between stakeholders
D. Ensures seller and buyer performance meet procurement requirements.

Answer:

B. Aligns internal & external stakeholder expectations
PMBOK® Guide Reference: 12.2
Process Group: Executing
Knowledge Area: Procurement

145. In identifying stakeholders, the expert judgment of all but which of the following groups should be sought?

A. Subject matter experts in the relevant area
B. Stakeholders with low interest and power scores
C. Industry groups and consultants
D. Senior management.

Answer:

B. Stakeholders with low interest and power scores
PMBOK® Guide Reference: 13.1.2.2
Process Group: Initiating
Knowledge Area: Stakeholder

146. Tools and techniques used to manage stakeholder engagement include:

A. Observation and project performance appraisals
B. Communication methods and interpersonal skills
C. Communication methods and information management systems
D. Expert judgment and meetings.

Answer:

B. Communication methods and interpersonal skills
PMBOK® Guide Reference: 13.3.2
Process Group: Executing
Knowledge Area: Stakeholder

147. Product Analysis and Alternatives Generation are two techniques used to:

A. Create a WBS
B. Collect Requirements
C. Define Scope
D. Define Activities.

Answer:

C. Define Scope
PMBOK® Guide Reference: 5.3.2
Process Group: Planning
Knowledge Area: Scope

148. You are running a project in an enterprise in which the project environment is one where the project manager's role is acknowledged, but you have low to moderate control. What type of project structure is this?

A. Balanced Matrix
B. Weak Matrix
C. Strong Matrix
D. Functional.

Answer:

A. Balanced Matrix
PMBOK® Guide Reference: 2.1.3, Table 2.1
Process Group: Executing
Knowledge Area: Human Resource Management

149. Control Scope:

A. Ensures that changes are processed through integrated change control
B. Helps to minimize scope creep
C. Is integrated with the other Control processes
D. All of the above.

Answer:

D. All of the above
PMBOK® Guide Reference: 5.6
Process Group: Monitoring & Controlling
Knowledge Area: Scope

150. Organizational process assets updated in controlling procurements include:

A. Correspondence and payment schedules
B. Risk and stakeholder registers
C. Record retention policies
D. Financial databases and completed checklists.

Answer:

A. Correspondence and payment schedules
PMBOK® Guide Reference: 12.3.3.5
Process Group: Monitoring & Control
Knowledge Area: Procurement

151. You have just inherited a project that was supposed to have generated 50,000 hours worth of value at this point, but has only generated 48,000 hours. You have burned 46,000 hours in the effort. Your project:

A. Is over budget and behind schedule
B. Is under budget and behind schedule
C. Is under budget and ahead of schedule
D. Is over budget and ahead of schedule.

Answer:

B. Is under budget and behind schedule
PMBOK® Guide Reference: 7.4.2; Table 7-1
Process Group: Monitoring & Controlling
Knowledge Area: Cost

152. Quality Assurance:

A. Is the process of monitoring & recording results of quality activities
B. Prevents defects via planning processes
C. Prevents defects via defect inspections
D. B and C.

Answer:

D. B and C
PMBOK® Guide Reference: 8.2
Process Group: Executing
Knowledge Area: Quality

153. Enterprise Environmental Factors include such items as:

A. Issue & defect management databases
B. Stakeholder risk tolerances
C. Project files from previous projects
D. A and B.

Answer:

B. Stakeholder risk tolerances (the other three are Organizational Process Assets).
PMBOK® Guide Reference: 4.3.1.3
Process Group: Executing
Knowledge Area: Integration

154. The type of information captured in a Stakeholder Register would include all but which of the following?

A. Stakeholder classification
B. Stakeholder communication requirements
C. Identification information
D. Assessment information.

Answer:

B. Stakeholder communication requirements
PMBOK® Guide Reference: 13.1.3.1
Process Group: Initiating
Knowledge Area: Stakeholder

155. The Manage Communications process allows for which of the following?

A. The ultimate disposition of project information
B. The appropriate generation of project information
C. Stakeholder requests for further clarification and discussion
D. All of the above.

Answer:

D. All of the above
PMBOK® Guide Reference: 10.2
Process Group: Executing
Knowledge Area: Communication

156. The Change Log that flows from the Integrated Change Control process:

A. Includes impacts in terms of risk to the project
B. Does not include information on rejected changes
C. Is for project team use only, and not typically shared with external stakeholders
D. A and B.

Answer:

A. Includes impacts in terms of risk to the project
PMBOK® Guide Reference: 4.5.3.2
Process Group: Monitoring & Control
Knowledge Area: Integration

157. A Requirements Management Plan includes:

A. A requirements prioritization process
B. Stakeholder requirements
C. Products metrics to be used
D. A and C.

Answer:

D. A and C
PMBOK® Guide Reference: 5.1.3.2
Process Group: Planning
Knowledge Area: Scope

158. Group Decision-Making Techniques include:

A. Plurality
B. Consensus
C. Collaboration
D. Compromise.

Answer:

A. Plurality
PMBOK® Guide Reference: 5.5.2.2
Process Group: Monitoring & Controlling
Knowledge Area: Scope

159. A primary difference in the use of Control Communications Tools & Techniques, versus Control Stakeholder Engagement, is that:

A. Information Management Systems are not used in Control Stakeholder Engagement
B. Expert Judgment doesn't call on industry groups / consultants in Cntl Communications
C. Meetings are focused on the project team with Control Communications, and on status review with Control Stakeholder Engagement
D. Interpersonal Skills are used in Cntl Commun, but not in Cntl Stkhlder Engagement.

Answer:

C. Meetings are focused on the project team with Control Communications, and on status review with Stakeholder Engagement
PMBOK® Guide Reference: 10.3.2.3, 13.4.2.3
Process Group: Monitoring & Control
Knowledge Area: Communications

160. You have just finished work on a document that includes a project scope statement, a WBS and a WBS dictionary. What have you just completed?

A. Performance Measurement Baseline
B. Requirements Document
C. SOW
D. Scope Baseline.

Answer:

D. Scope Baseline
PMBOK® Guide Reference: 5.4.3.1
Process Group: Planning
Knowledge Area: Scope

161. Analytical techniques that may be used in planning schedule management include all but which of the following?

A. Choosing estimating approaches
B. Detailing processes for fast-tracking & crashing
C. Choosing scheduling methodologies or tools
D. Variance Analysis.

Answer:

D. Variance Analysis
PMBOK® Guide Reference: 6.1.2.2
Process Group: Planning
Knowledge Area: Time

162. In addition to information in the register, the stakeholder management plan provides:

A. Roles and responsibilities
B. Reason for distribution of stakeholder information
C. Methods used to convey information
D. B and C.

Answer:

B. Reason for distribution of stakeholder information
PMBOK® Guide Reference: 13.2.3.1
Process Group: Planning
Knowledge Area: Stakeholder

163. Quality Control inputs include which of the following?

A. Process improvement plan
B. Work performance information
C. Quality metrics & checklists
D. Change Requests.

Answer:

C. Quality metrics & checklists
PMBOK® Guide Reference: 8.3.1
Process Group: Monitoring & Control
Knowledge Area: Quality

164. Manage Stakeholder Engagement outputs include:

A. Enterprise Environmental Factors & Change Requests
B. Project Communication & Document Updates
C. Issue Log & Change Requests
D. Work Performance Information & Change Requests.

Answer:

C. Issue Log & Change Requests
PMBOK® Guide Reference: 13.3.3
Process Group: Executing
Knowledge Area: Stakeholder

165. Dependency attributes include:

A. Mandatory or Discretionary
B. Fixed or Variable
C. Internal or External
D. A and C.

Answer:

D. A and C
PMBOK® Guide Reference: 6.3.2.2
Process Group: Planning
Knowledge Area: Time

166. Organizational process assets updated by the Controlling Stakeholders process include:

A. Project or phase closure documents
B. Scope, cost & schedule baselines
C. Project presentations and reports
D. A and B.

Answer:

C. Project presentations and reports
PMBOK® Guide Reference: 13.4.3.5
Process Group: Monitoring & Control
Knowledge Area: Stakeholder

167. A good project management plan (as opposed to project documents) includes:

A. A Change Management Plan
B. Project Calendars
C. Team Performance Assessments
D. A and B.

Answer:

A. A Change Management Plan
PMBOK® Guide Reference: 4.2.3.1, Table 4-1
Process Group: Planning
Knowledge Area: Integration

168. You are working on identifying project requirements. You decide to use a technique that enhances brainstorming with a voting process. You have chosen:

A. Idea/Mind Mapping
B. Nominal Group Technique
C. An Affinity Diagram
D. Multicriteria Decision Analysis.

Answer:

B. Nominal Group Technique
PMBOK® Guide Reference: 5.2.2.4
Process Group: Planning
Knowledge Area: Scope

169. When implementing risk contingency plans, what type of chng requests can result?

A. Recommended corrective actions
B. Recommended preventive actions
C. A and B
D. None of the above.

Answer:

C. A and B
PMBOK® Guide Reference: 11.6.3.2
Process Group: Monitoring & Control
Knowledge Area: Risk

170. You are project managing a team with a total size of 15 members, including you. A week ago, additional critical scope was added that will require you adding 5 members to your team to meet your date commitment, which will not be relaxed. How many communication channels are you adding to the team?

A. 90
B. 85
C. 105
D. 190.

Answer:

B. 85; Channels presently equal (15(15-1))/2, or 105. Adding 5 members to the team moves that number to ((20(20-1))/2, or 190. 190 minus 105 equals 85.
PMBOK® Guide Reference: 10.1.2.1
Process Group: Planning
Knowledge Area: Communication

171. Team performance evaluation indicators include

A. Reduced turnover
B. Improvements in skills & competencies
C. Increased sharing of information
D. All of the above.

Answer:

D. All of the above
PMBOK® Guide Reference: 9.3.3.1
Process Group: Executing
Knowledge Area: Human Resource Management

172. You have been appointed to a team tasked with project selection for the enterprise. In making project selections, which of the following criteria is most critical?

A. Potential benefits to be realized by the enterprise
B. Balancing cost-saving and revenue-producing projects
C. ROI
D. Realism.

Answer:

D. Realism
PMBOK® Guide Reference: No specific reference. All of the criteria listed are important, but none are more important than selecting projects that have a realistic chance to succeed.
Process Group: Initiating
Knowledge Area: Integration

173. Quality Management and Control tools unique to assurance activities include:

A. Matrix Diagrams & Prioritization Matrices
B. Cause & Effect Diagrams
C. Pareto Diagrams
D. Control Charts.

Answer:

A. Matrix Diagrams & Prioritization Matrices
PMBOK® Guide Reference: 8.2.2.1
Process Group: Executing
Knowledge Area: Quality

174. The Stakeholder Register:

A. Can be discarded once the Risk Register is produced
B. Is produced one time, at project initiation
C. Should be shared freely with all stakeholders listed
D. Should be consulted regularly, as stakeholders may change during the project.

Answer:

D. Should be consulted regularly, as stakeholders may change during the project
PMBOK® Guide Reference: 13.1
Process Group: Initiating
Knowledge Area: Stakeholder

175. Tools and techniques used in controlling procurements include:

A. Expert judgment and analytical techniques
B. Procurement negotiations and independent estimates
C. Payment systems and claims administration
D. Market research and meetings.

Answer:

C. Payment systems and claims administration
PMBOK® Guide Reference: 12.3.2
Process Group: Monitoring & Control
Knowledge Area: Procurement

176. You have decided to use the critical chain method to manage your project. Your concern is focused right now on managing three non-critical chains in your project network. You are considering:

A. Adding a project buffer to your network
B. Adding feeding buffers to the three non-critical chains
C. Managing the free float on your non-critical chains
D. Managing the total float on your non-critical chains.

Answer:

B. Adding feeding buffers to the three non-critical chains
PMBOK® Guide Reference: 6.6.2.3
Process Group: Planning
Knowledge Area: Time

177. Configuration Management activities include all but which of the following:

A. Configuration identification
B. Configuration status accounting
C. Configuration scope creep control
D. Configuration verification/audit.

Answer:

C. Configuration scope creep control
PMBOK® Guide Reference: 4.5
Process Group: Monitoring & Control
Knowledge Area: Integration

178. Motivational Pioneer Abraham Maslow is typically associated with:

A. Theory X & Theory Y
B. Expectancy Theory
C. A Pyramid-shaped Hierarchy of Needs
D. Theory Z.

Answer:

C. A Pyramid-shaped Hierarchy of Needs
PMBOK® Guide Reference: No specific reference. Know your motivational pioneers!
Process Group: Executing
Knowledge Area: Human Resource Management

179. You are considering bidding on a project that could be a real growth stimulator for your enterprise, but your limited capital resources just won't stretch to meet the requirements. You are considering entering into a joint venture with a larger company that you have partnered with in the past, and that has better capital resources at their disposal. What type of risk response strategy is this?

A. Mitigation
B. Transference
C. Sharing
D. Enhancement.

Answer:

C. Sharing
PMBOK® Guide Reference: 11.5.2.2
Process Group: Planning
Knowledge Area: Risk

180. Organizational Process Assets Updates Outputs of the Close Project or Phase Process include which of the following?

A. Closed procurements
B. Final product, service or result transition
C. Project or phase closure documents
D. Procurement files.

Answer:

C. Project or phase closure documents
PMBOK® Guide Reference: 4.6.3
Process Group: Closing
Knowledge Area: Integration

181. In planning procurements, which of the following might be used as source selection criteria?

A. Warranty proposed and business size/type
B. Life cycle costs and financial capacity
C. Management approach and understanding of need
D. All of the above.

Answer:

D. All of the above
PMBOK® Guide Reference: 12.1.3.4
Process Group: Planning
Knowledge Area: Procurement

182. Tools & Techniques used to control schedules include

A. Critical path method
B. Variance analysis
C. Reserve Analysis
D. Inspection.

Answer:

A. Critical path method
PMBOK® Guide Reference: 6.7.2.1
Process Group: Monitoring & Control
Knowledge Area: Time

183. You are Closing Procurements. What are you producing?

A. Project files & phase closure documents
B. Change requests and work performance information
C. Stakeholder notifications and feedback
D. The Procurement file & deliverable acceptance.

Answer:

D. Procurement file & deliverable acceptance
PMBOK® Guide Reference: 12.4.3.2
Process Group: Closing
Knowledge Area: Procurements

184. Three-Point Estimating:

A. Is synonymous with PERT
B. May use either a Beta or Triangular Distribution
C. Uses most likely, least likely and somewhat unlikely estimates in its formulas
D. None of the above.

Answer:

B. May use either a Beta or Triangular Distribution
PMBOK® Guide Reference: 7.2.2.5
Process Group: Planning
Knowledge Area: Cost

185. The Human Resource Management Plan includes:

A. Methods or Technologies used to convey information
B. Stakeholder Interrelationships
C. Roles & Responsibilities information
D. A and C.

Answer:

C. Roles & Responsibilities information
PMBOK® Guide Reference: 9.1.3.1
Process Group: Planning
Knowledge Area: Human Resource Management

186. Performance reporting is critical for a project. It involves:

A. Collecting & analyzing baseline versus actual data
B. Providing information at the appropriate level for each audience
C. A and B
D. None of the above.

Answer:

C. A and B
PMBOK® Guide Reference: 10.2.2.5
Process Group: Executing
Knowledge Area: Communication

187. A Cost Management Plan includes all but which of the following?

A. Rules of performance measurement & control thresholds
B. Level of accuracy & units of measure information
C. Procedures for project cost reporting
D. Project schedule model information.

Answer:

D. Project schedule model information
PMBOK® Guide Reference: 7.1.3.1
Process Group: Planning
Knowledge Area: Cost

188. When developing a project team, which tools might you use?

A. Networking & organizational theory
B. Negotiation & Multi-Criteria Decision Analysis
C. Team-Building activities & personnel assessment tools
D. Observation & Conversation.

Answer:

C. Team-Building activities & personnel assessment tools
PMBOK® Guide Reference: 9.3.2
Process Group: Executing
Knowledge Area: Human Resource Management

189. A type of audit that identifies nonconforming organizational/project processes is:

A. Procurement Audit
B. Quality Audit
C. Risk Audit
D. Tax Audit.

Answer:

B. Quality Audit
PMBOK® Guide Reference: 8.2.2.2
Process Group: Executing
Knowledge Area: Quality

190. You have just been hired by your company on the basis of your project management certification and years of experience. You have been placed in charge of a critical project. Which power type are you most likely to use?

A. Authoritarian
B. Referent
C. Expert
D. Legitimate.

Answer:

D. Legitimate
PMBOK® Guide Reference: No specific reference. You have to prove your expertise!
Process Group: Executing
Knowledge Area: Human Resource Management

191. If your project has passed the halfway point with respect to calendar, its CPI is .65, and your SPI is also less than 1.0, you should:

A. Begin replanning efforts, as your original estimates were flawed
B. Begin working to improve productivity and thereby increase your CPI
C. Investigate the impact that maintenance costs are having on your project
D. Work to improve your SPI, as improvements in SPI should have a positive effect on your CPI.

Answer:

A. Begin replanning efforts, as your original estimates were flawed
PMBOK® Guide Reference: No specific reference; CPI less than .8 is generally unrecoverable
Process Group: Monitoring & Controlling
Knowledge Area: Cost

192. In acquiring project team resources, the project management team will typically negotiate with which of the following?

E. Functional managers and other project teams
F. Government regulators
G. Industry groups specializing in estimating or risk
H. Legal experts.

Answer:

A. Functional managers and other project teams
PMBOK® Guide Reference: 9.2.2.2
Process Group: Executing
Knowledge Area: Human Resource Management

193. In understanding communication management tools, it is important to know that:

A. A primary focus of communication models is to identify & manage barriers
B. A primary focus of communication technology is to identify & manage barriers
C. A primary focus of communication methods is to identify & manage barriers
D. A primary focus of communication models is to ensure information is received and understood.

Answer:

A. A primary focus of communication models is to identify & manage barriers
PMBOK® Guide Reference: 10.2.2
Process Group: Executing
Knowledge Area: Communication

194. Changes can be:

A. Corrective or Preventive in nature
B. A planned workaround
C. Defect repairs
D. A and C.

Answer:

D. A and C. A workaround is, by definition (P 567), not a planned event.
PMBOK® Guide Reference: 4.3
Process Group: Executing
Knowledge Area: Integration

195. Organizational process assets updated while managing stakeholder engagement include:

A. Project reports and presentations
B. Project records and lessons learned
C. Stakeholder notifications and feedback
D. All of the above.

Answer:

D. All of the above
PMBOK® Guide Reference: 13.3.3.5
Process Group: Executing
Knowledge Area: Stakeholder

196. Use of analytical techniques within the context of conducting procurements can identify:

A. Areas that call for closer monitoring
B. Root cause and project performance forecasts
C. Estimating approaches or optimal financial techniques to employ
D. Overall risk exposure.

Answer:

A. Areas that call for closer monitoring
PMBOK® Guide Reference: 12.2.2.6
Process Group: Executing
Knowledge Area: Procurement

197. Stakeholders are typically classified as:

A. Supportive or resistant
B. Existing or future
C. Management or non-management
D. Technical or non-technical.

Answer:

A. Supportive or resistant
PMBOK® Guide Reference: 13.1.3.1
Process Group: Initiating
Knowledge Area: Stakeholder

198. Procurements Negotiations:

A. Employs litigation as its preferred option
B. Sometimes involves mediation or arbitration
C. Is more concerned with the letter of the contract than equitable settlement
D. A and C.

Answer:

B. Sometimes involves mediation or arbitration
PMBOK® Guide Reference: 12.4.2.2
Process Group: Closing
Knowledge Area: Procurements

199. You are the project manager of a project that has just completed the concept, or ideation, phase. What are the key artifacts of this phase?

A. Project Plan and WBS
B. Stakeholder Register and Project Charter
C. Communication and Stakeholder Management Plans
D. A and B.

Answer:

B. Stakeholder Register and Project Charter
PMBOK® Guide Reference: 4.1.3.1; 13.1.3.1
Process Group: Initiating
Knowledge Area: Integration & Stakeholder

200. Administrative closure of a project includes all but which of the following?

A. Actions necessary to satisfy exit criteria
B. Actions needed to process any early termination of a project contract
C. Actions needed to collect project records
D. Activities necessary to transfer the project's products to their next phase or operations.

Answer:

B. Actions needed to process any early termination of a project contract
PMBOK® Guide Reference: 4.6
Process Group: Closing
Knowledge Area: Integration

Sample PMP Exam®

Question	Answer	Key Domain	Knowledge Area
1	D	Closing	Integration
2	B	Initiating	Integration
3	B	Closing	Procurement
4	D	Initiating	Stakeholder
5	A	Executing	Procurement
6	C	Executing	Stakeholder
7	D	Executing	Integration
8	D	Executing	Communication
9	C	Executing	Human Resources
10	C	M & C	Cost
11	B	Executing	Human Resources
12	A	Executing	Quality
13	B	Executing	Human Resources
14	D	M & C	Integration
15	D	M & C	Quality
16	B	M & C	Procurement
17	A	M & C	Integration
18	B	M & C	Communication
19	C	M & C	Scope
20	D	M & C	Risk
21	B	Planning	Time
22	D	M & C	Stakeholder
23	B	M & C	Scope
24	A	Planning	Stakeholder
25	A	Planning	Time
26	C	Planning	Procurement
27	B	Planning	Human Resources
28	C	Planning	Risk
29	C	Planning	Integration
30	B	Planning	Scope
31	B	Planning	Risk
32	C	Planning	Time
33	D	Planning	Cost
34	C	Planning	Scope
35	D	Planning	Risk
36	A	Planning	Communication
37	A	Planning	Scope
38	C	Planning	Time
39	A	Planning	Quality
40	B	Planning	Scope
41	D	Initiating	Integration
42	D	Executing	Procurement
43	A	Initiating	Stakeholder
44	D	Executing	Stakeholder
45	C	Closing	Procurement
46	D	Executing	Human Resources
47	B	Executing	Integration
48	D	Executing	Human Resources
49	A	Closing	Integration
50	B	Planning	Time
51	D	Planning	Time
52	C	Executing	Quality
53	A	Executing	Human Resources
54	B	Executing	Communication
55	D	Planning	Risk
56	D	M & C	Integration
57	A	M & C	Communication
58	C	Initiating	Stakeholder
59	D	Initiating	Integration
60	C	Planning	Time
61	A	M & C	Procurement
62	B	Executing	Stakeholder
63	A	M & C	Scope
64	A	M & C	Quality
65	A	Executing	Human Resources
66	C	Executing	Integration
67	C	M & C	Integration
68	A	Planning	Scope
69	A	M & C	Risk
70	B	M & C	Scope
71	C	Executing	Communication
72	C	Closing	Integration
73	C	Initiating	Stakeholder
74	D	Initiating	Integration
75	C	Executing	Procurement

Question	Answer	Key Domain	Knowledge Area
76	D	Closing	Procurement
77	B	Executing	Quality
78	A	Executing	Human Resources
79	B	Planning	Scope
80	C	M & C	Integration
81	A	Initiating	Integration
82	C	Planning	Time
83	B	Planning	Cost
84	D	M & C	Quality
85	D	M & C	Procurement
86	A	M & C	Stakeholder
87	A	M & C	Cost
88	B	Executing	Integration
89	B	Executing	Communication
90	B	Executing	Human Resources
91	A	Executing	Stakeholder
92	B	Executing	Human Resources
93	D	Closing	Integration
94	C	Executing	Procurement
95	A	Closing	Procurement
96	C	Initiating	Stakeholder
97	D	Initiating	Integration
98	B	M & C	Integration
99	B	M & C	Cost
100	D	M & C	Cost
101	C	M & C	Cost
102	D	M & C	Cost
103	A	Initiating	Stakeholder
104	D	Initiating	Integration
105	A	Executing	Stakeholder
106	C	Executing	Quality
107	B	Initiating	Stakeholder
108	C	Closing	Procurement
109	A	Executing	Human Resources
110	A	Executing	Communication
111	A	Planning	Risk
112	B	M & C	Risk
113	D	M & C	Scope
114	C	Executing	Human Resources
115	C	Planning	Communication
116	A	M & C	Integration
117	B	Executing	Integration
118	C	Initiating	Integration
119	D	M & C	Communication
120	C	M & C	Scope
121	C	Planning	Time
122	B	M & C	Quality
123	A	Closing	Procurement
124	B	Executing	Procurement
125	B	Planning	Time
126	D	Planning	Time
127	D	Initiating	Stakeholder
128	D	Initiating	Integration
129	D	Executing	Human Resources
130	B	Planning	Quality
131	C	Planning	Risk
132	D	M & C	Stakeholder
133	D	Initiating	Stakeholder
134	D	Executing	Procurement
135	D	Planning	Time
136	D	Initiating	Integration
137	B	Planning	Risk
138	C	Executing	Human Resources
139	A	Closing	Integration
140	D	Executing	Integration
141	D	Closing	Procurement
142	D	Executing	Human Resources
143	B	Initiating	Integration
144	B	Executing	Procurement
145	B	Initiating	Stakeholder
146	B	Executing	Stakeholder
147	C	Planning	Scope
148	A	Executing	Human Resources
149	D	M & C	Scope
150	A	M & C	Procurement

Question	Answer	Key Domain	Knowledge Area
151	B	M & C	Cost
152	D	Executing	Quality
153	B	Executing	Integration
154	B	Initiating	Stakeholder
155	D	Executing	Communication
156	A	M & C	Integration
157	D	Planning	Scope
158	A	M & C	Scope
159	C	M & C	Communication
160	D	Planning	Scope
161	D	Planning	Time
162	B	Planning	Stakeholder
163	C	M & C	Quality
164	C	Executing	Stakeholder
165	D	Planning	Time
166	C	M & C	Stakeholder
167	A	Planning	Integration
168	B	Planning	Scope
169	C	M & C	Risk
170	B	Planning	Communication
171	D	Executing	Human Resources
172	D	Initiating	Integration
173	A	Executing	Quality
174	D	Initiating	Stakeholder
175	C	M & C	Procurement
176	B	Planning	Time
177	C	M & C	Integration
178	C	Executing	Human Resources
179	C	Planning	Risk
180	C	Closing	Integration
181	D	Planning	Procurement
182	A	M & C	Time
183	D	Closing	Procurement
184	B	Planning	Cost
185	C	Planning	Human Resources
186	C	Executing	Communication
187	D	Planning	Cost
188	C	Executing	Human Resources
189	B	Executing	Quality
190	D	Executing	Human Resources
191	A	M & C	Cost
192	A	Executing	Human Resources
193	A	Executing	Communication
194	D	Executing	Integration
195	D	Executing	Stakeholder
196	A	Executing	Procurement
197	A	Initiating	Stakeholder
198	B	Closing	Procurement
199	B	Initiating	Integration
200	B	Closing	Integration

About the Author

With over 30 years' experience in software development, program management and project management, Mr. Tracy has managed over 100 major projects for national and international corporations and public sector entities. In the private sector, his responsibilities have ranged from software developer and development manager to project manager and project/program director, managing over $50 million in software projects annually. In the public sector, John has served as Chief Information Officer of a very large school district, directing major software, network, hardware and data center initiatives. He has also done senior level PM consulting work for public and private sector clients both domestically and internationally.

Over the past 12 years, Mr. Tracy has developed and delivered online and traditional project management training for educational and public institutions as well as private corporations. He holds Masters Degrees in Business Administration and Management Information Systems, has held continuous PMP certification since 1998, and is currently engaged in developing and delivering project management courseware and senior level consulting. His first book, "A Project Manager's Storybook (With Cases)" was published in 2012.